PIONEERING PARSIS OF CALCUTTA

PROCHY N MEHTA

NIYOGI BOOKS

Published by
NIYOGI BOOKS
Block D, Building No. 77,
Okhla Industrial Area, Phase-I,
New Delhi-110 020, INDIA
Tel: 91-11-26816301, 26818960
Email: niyogibooks@gmail.com
Website: www.niyogibooksindia.com

Editor: Sucharita Ghosh
Design: Shashi Bhushan Prasad
Cover Image: Sketch by Swaroop Mukerji

ISBN: 978-93-89136-42-5
Publication: 2020
Reprint: 2025

Printed at: Niyogi Offset Pvt. Ltd., New Delhi, India

Index

CONTENTS

FOREWORD

I consider it a privilege and an honour to be asked to write this Foreword to Prochy N Mehta's discourse, very apty named *Pioneering Parsis of Calcutta*.

Prochy needs no introduction to anyone in Calcutta, more known to all of us as an icon in the sphere of athletics, who has brought honour and glory to the country at the national and international levels, and made the community so very proud of her achievements.

What has come as a pleasant surprise to me, and I am sure to many others, is her talent and dedication as a research scholar, who has burnt a lot of midnight oil and toiled for many an hour to bring out this book. The in-depth study she has done to bring out every facet in such detail, makes it difficult to even imagine the quantum of effort and hard work she has put in over a period of almost two years. Pursuit of perfection has been her goal and she has achieved it by her determination and dedication.

To me, it is her *obsession* which has resulted in her commitment and dedication to the cause of highlighting the glorious achievements of the pioneer Parsis who came to Calcutta under the most difficult conditions, and achieved recognition and greatness, leaving behind a legacy of which we are the beneficiaries today.

Much as we owe each and every one of them a debt of gratitude, they would, in time to come (if not already), be just names and no more. It is to Prochy's credit and due to her perseverance that the community has been enlightened and made aware of the trials and tribulations that they had to go through before earning glory and fame.

The community today and more so, posterity tomorrow, have to be grateful to Prochy for this *must-read* history of the Calcutta Parsis which is a mine of wealth and truly a labour of love.

Noshir Tankariwala
Trustee
Late Ervad D.B. Mehta's Zoroastrian Anjuman Atash Adaran

PREFACE

All journeys have a beginning; a moment at which a decision is made or a first step taken. For me that moment came when my granddaughter, a child whose Navjote had been performed, was refused permission to enter our religious place of worship on the premise that she was not a Parsi. All personal feelings aside, I felt that that could not be the stance that a progressive faith that prided itself on its forward-thinking philosophy, not to mention the high rate of education, should adopt. I also felt that somewhere, at some time, there must have been other Parsis who had faced this discrimination and wondered what the verdict would have been during those times.

As a practising Parsi, I have to confess I am not deeply religious. Nor did I really study my religion or its tenets. For all of us, it has been a matter of taking what we were taught on faith and then carrying on the tradition. I felt that the time had come to change that. But change requires knowledge and proof, and reasonable basis for an argument. So, to do that, I turned to research. Thus began my journey towards the truth.

I had no illusions. What I was taking on is what every religion faces at some stage: the fear of change. Any change from the norm upsets someone or the other. Sometimes change comes about because there are enough people to force the change through. Sometimes the silent majority want the change but do not have the time, means or patience to make it come about. I felt I had all three. More importantly, I wouldn't allow my daughter's children to be treated any differently than the children of my son.

The research was illuminating. A trip down the past showed the Parsi community in a vastly different light. As part of my research I came across those intrepid men who had left settled homes in the west to journey to Calcutta to start a new life with their partners. I came across men who made millions and lost it all and started again. Men who changed professions several times before achieving success. Those who prospered academically and those who prospered through astute decisions and gambling on what constitutes a sunrise and sunset industry. I realised that the Parsis of old were much more forward-looking and had fought publicly to resolve issues where the majority was unwilling to give the resurgent minority its way. It helped that the reformists were wealthy, influential people in their own right who had the knowledge and wisdom to know that change was coming. And needed to come.

The truth is there for all to see. As early as 1908 the Petit Vs Jeejeebhoy case was filed to allow people who had married Parsis to have access to the grants and funds that were available to all other Parsis on the plea that they were now part of the community. In 1914, Dastur Kaikobad Aderbad Dastur Noshirwan, Head Priest of the Deccan and the D.B. Mehta Anjuman, journeyed to Rangoon to perform the Navjote of Bella, the daughter of a non-Parsi gentleman and his Parsi wife, who was later adopted by a Parsi gentleman and his non-Parsi wife (who herself later got converted, became a Parsi and married the gentleman in question). A similar set of high-ranking priests performed the marriage ceremony of Susaune Briere (a French national) to Ratanji Dadabhoy Tata, after allowing her to don the mantle of being a Parsi through a Navjote ceremony, followed immediately after by the wedding at the Sethna house in Bombay.

Nor were these stray, clandestine affairs conducted on the sly. All of these ceremonies were performed in full view of a range of witnesses (the Susaune Briere marriage had sixty of the best priests in the community attending). The newspapers of those times came up strongly for and against this breach of custom. Defamation suits were filed by those who were pilloried by the press. The battles took place in the significant glare of media publicity with the newspapers (who opposed the change) asking their readers for support to fight this new change to the rules. The plaintiffs were men of high learning and culture, vaunted members of the community, and they did not shy away from the fight either. The clashes raged. The press had to back down and pay for damages. It was full-on drama fought during the turn of the century.

I present here the findings of these cases. What was alleged against those who stood for change, what was argued, what was lost ... and what was won. Along the way I came across the great Parsis of the times and was advised that writing about them could help the community as well.

So here is the summary of what I found. Knowledge that we can now all have access to. More than anything else, I hope it will help us remember that change is inevitable.

And that this book will help us never to forget.

ANCIENT HISTORY

In ancient times, Zoroastrians referred to themselves as 'Marzdayasna'. In the Islamic period another designation became popular – Zartost or Zarthost – and eventually the Gujarati word 'Jarousti', now Zoroastrian. Both these nomenclatures come from *Yasna* 12.1 – primary collection of religious texts of Zoroastrianism in the Avestan language in the *Gathas* – which begins thus: 'I profess myself a worshipper, a follower of Zarathustra'.

Trade and cultural relations existed between Iran and India in the Sasanian age (224-651 CE). There is a reference to the 'Parasikas' in the *Mahabharata*, the Puranas and the *Raghuvamsa* of Kalidas. There is mention of the Parthaya or Parthians in inscriptions found in Nasik, Girnar and Karli. As early as 126 BCE, the Parthian King Meander is said to have had suzerainty in Sourashtra.

Parsis supposedly came to India in 636 CE, to escape Arab persecution. At that time, we came along already established trade routes and there was a considerable Parsi population existing in this area along the banks of the Sind. There is no recorded history of our arrival in India, only an epic poem called '*Kissa-e-Sanjan*' written by a Parsi priest, Baman Kaikobad, in 1599 (963 years after the exodus from Iran). It is written in poetic style going back and forth in time.

Till the early 1700s, when the British came to India, the Parsis existed as a tribe amongst the Hindus following many Hindu customs and procedures. With the coming of the British and the Parsis' great involvement in trade with China, new wealth came to our community. It is at this time that we started building our fire temples (places of worship) and dokhmas (funeral practices).

The erudite author Sorabji Mancherji Desai of the *Tawarikh-e-Navsari* writes that around 1490

> ... with their prolonged stay with the Hindus, the Parsis had become almost like them. The males used to put red pagdis and dhotis. Their names were mostly Hindu names such as Hasji, Fakir, Jogia, Narsang and Dhana. The ladies had such names as Malanbai, Zilibai, Dhanabai. They used to dress and put on decorative ornaments like those of Hindu ladies. The then Parsis even used wooden biers for carrying the dead and used to help in carrying the corpses. Changasha helped in preserving the rich Parsi heritage and after first satisfying the economic needs of the indigent Parsis from the neighbouring villages, he started restoring their faith in their glorious ancient religion and put them on the right religious path.

The well-known French traveller and scholar Abraham Hyacinthe Anquetil-Duperron wrote the following about Changasha:

> There appeared afterwards at Navsari, a rich Parsi named Changasha, a faithful observer of the Zoroastrian law. He distributed his wealth among the poor, provided the Parsis with *kustis* and *sudras* and endeavoured to bring back those whom ignorance and trouble had led into many errors to the exact practice of the Zoroastrian law. To succeed in this, he applied to the Dastoors of Kerman, consulting them on different points of the Zoroastrian religion, neglected in Gujarat.

This was the beginning of the Rivayats, questions sent to Iran to seek answers on religion.

It was at the end of the eighteenth century that Sir William Jones, a judge in the Presidency of Bengal, originally reported striking similarities between Sanskrit, Greek and Latin. This helped scholars (the most famous of which were Lawrence Mills, Jackson and Martin Haug) to translate our *Gatha*s.

Haug was a professor of Sanskrit in Poona Government College. He inspired the younger generation of Parsis to take an interest in their own sacred scriptures. His book *Essays on the Sacred Language, Writings and Religion of the Parsis* (1862) offered the first grammatical description of the Avestan language in comparison with Sanskrit. He translated two volumes of the *Gatha*s, published over 1858-1860.

His lasting contribution to Iranian studies includes the discovery that the language of the *Gatha*s is different from that of the rest of the *Avesta* and that only the *Gatha*s were composed by Zarathustra. In his lecture in Bombay, Haug argued that Zarathustra taught a pure, ethical monotheism, that there was no evidence for rituals in the *Gatha*s and that the prophet's teachings were corrupted by later generations. Haug was assisted by Dastur Hoshang Jamaspji (High Priest of the Deccan).

Lawrence Mills translated the *Gatha*s in 1887. He was professor of Zend Philology of the Persian language. He translated the *Gatha*s into English. In 1911 *The Parsi*, Bombay (weekly edition) noted 'the debt of Parsis to Professor Mills' for translating the *Gatha*s into English.

The first Parsi who came to Calcutta around 1767 was Dadabhai Behramji Banaji. Parsis used to trade with Armenian brokers in Surat. These Armenians came to Murshidabad and thence to Calcutta. It is possible that some Parsi traders may have accompanied these Armenians, first to Murshidabad and then Calcutta. Many of the Parsi families that first settled in Calcutta did so around the Armenian localities.

FIRST PARSIS TO SETTLE IN CALCUTTA (1780 ONWARDS)

For almost 900 years, Zoroastrians lived in India as a tribe amongst the local people. With the opium trade with China, came new affluence. In the early 1800s, Zoroastrians relearnt their religion and started establishing places of worship and dokhmas for funeral rites. In this chapter we discuss the pioneering spirit of these Parsis and the hardships they bore to come and settle in a new area to build a community.

Meherwanji Tabak was a well-known Parsi living in Calcutta around 1780-1790. He had a thriving trading business. Unfortunately, little is recorded about him in official records or books, except that Sir Jamshedjee Jeejeebhoy started his career as a clerk in Meherwanji Tabak's trading house in Calcutta.

Sir Jamshedjee Jeejeebhoy, first baronet Jeejeebhoy of Bombay (1783-1859), started his career in Bombay as a dealer in bottles. He came to Calcutta in 1799 and worked as a clerk in Meherwanji Tabak's trading house. Tabak was his cousin and employed him at a salary of Rs 2 per month. Jamshedjee went to China with Meherwanji Tabak to start an opium trade. His first two trips resulted in heavy losses. On his third trip, the ship in which he was travelling was waylaid by pirates and he was later released in South Africa. From there he managed to find his way back to Serampore, penniless and starving. In 1807 he made his fourth trip to China which turned out to be a success. He amassed huge wealth and gave extensively to charity.

Sir Jamshedjee Jeejeebhoy

During the Bengal famine of 1943, an English journal observed: 'The vast contributions made by the leading businessman, Seth Jamshedjee Jeejeebhoy, towards the Bengal Famine Fund has put to shame many Bengali Babus who are wealthier than him.'

Nusserwanji Cawasji Petit arrived in Bombay in 1785 from Surat and established a business as a ship agent and chandler. Nusserwanji came in close contact with the French in India who called him 'Petit' because of his diminutive stature. This name eventually became his surname. He opened a branch of his business in Calcutta but it was not very successful. He came to Calcutta to manage the estate of his father-in-law, Jamshedji Kukajee Majaina.

Honorary Sir Dinshaw Maneckji Petit was appointed a member of the Viceroy's Legislative Council in 1888 by the British Government. He donated Rs 7,000 to the Calcutta Zoroastrian Community's Religious & Charity Fund to establish a library. He hosted the dinner

Sir Dinshaw Maneckji Petit
Photo courtesy: Parsiana Publications

for the Zoroastrian Conference where Dastur Kaikobad Aderbad Dastur Noshirwan spoke about the universality of the Zoroastrian religion and that it was meant for all mankind.

Jamshedji Kukajee Majaina set up trade links with Ceylon, Calcutta and China via Madras. Settling down in Calcutta in 1793, he died on 10 March 1810, the first Parsi to die in Calcutta. His son-in-law, Nusserwanji Cawasji Petit, came to Calcutta to manage his estate. He donated large properties to Parsis living in Calcutta.

Navroji Sorabji Umrigar was the son of Sorabji Jagiji Umrigar. Moving about in palanquins was in vogue in Bombay in those days and Sorabji made this his living. At the time it was the custom to stock grain and provisions for the whole year. It was on one of those occasions, when Sorabji set out to make his annual purchase, that he had a brilliant idea. Instead of going to the market, he went directly to the vernacular school where young Navroji was studying. Turning a deaf ear to the teacher's entreaties to continue Navroji's Gujarati education, he took him to a seminary run by an Englishman in a quarter of the town known as English Bazar. There he disclosed the purpose of his visit. It was to entreat the Englishman to teach his son English as long as he could, with the money he had brought with him.

As Sorabji neared his house without stores or cash, the jubilance gradually gave way to a sober review of the situation. The reception by his wife Ratanbai when she found out what he had done was none too cordial and interspersed with sarcastic sallies for which she was noted. In later years when the tide of their fortune had turned, she would never fail to extol to her friends the wisdom of her husband nor forgive herself for feeding him only salt and bread for forty days.

Navroji learnt English and also the traits of the English character. At twenty, he made two voyages to China and was appointed Native Agent at Calcutta of the firm Sir Charles Forbes in 1807. He had a prosperous career as a merchant. He was given the surname 'Bengalee' during his long residence in Calcutta. He had two sons: Shapurji and Dadabhoy.

In 1822 he built the first Tower of Silence at a cost of Rs 35,000 and, three years later, when he died at the age of forty-five, his was the first body to be placed in the Tower of Silence. His faithful dog who had followed the cortège, refused all food and drink after returning from the funeral and died within three or four days of his death.

After his death, his son Shapurji handled his estate. He built a Sagri near the Tower of Silence in memory of his father.

The *Parsi Prakash,* Vol. I (1860) states:

> 28th January 1822, Roz Asman 27, Mah 4 (Tir) 119 1 Y.Z. Today a Tower of Silence built at his own expense by a Calcutta merchant, Seth Navroji Sorabjee Umrigar, was duly consecrated.
>
> We have seen a photograph in the possession of Seth Sorabji Shapoorji Bengali, a relation of Seth Navroji, from which it appears the area surrounding the Tower of Silence has been

The Tower of Silence built at Calcutta by Sorabji's grandfather Navroji Sorabji Umrigar (Bengalee), 28th January 1822

Entrance to the Tower of Silence built by Sorabji's grandfather Navroji Sorabji Umrigar (Bengalee)

enclosed with a high wall and the Tower of Silence has been built on one side. This was the property of the Calcutta Parsi Anjuman and prior to the construction of this Tower of Silence, the Parsi dead were buried there. The burial place is carefully maintained a little beyond the Tower of Silence. Two plaques have been fixed on the outer wall of the compound of the Tower of Silence.

In the name of Dadar Ahuramazda Roz 27 Asman, Mah 4 Tir, year 1191 Yezdezardi
Indian year 1878, Mah sood 4 Monday, 28th January 1822

For the use and benefit of the Parsee Community, the followers of the good religion of Zarathustra, we have with our own efforts and with the Grace of God, constructed this resting place. It is incumbent on the future Parsees to take due care of the place and the Tower of Silence.

(Translation of the first plaque, originally in Gujarati)

Parsi Nowrojee Sorabjee Umrigar Burial ground of the Parsis purchased by their voluntary subscription and surrounded with a wall, at the expense and under the superintendence of Nowrojee Sorabjee

Erected in Calcutta 28th January 1822

(Translation of the second plaque, originally in Gujarati)

An interesting episode connecting Calcutta with Modi Atash Behram in Surat

In Surat, Bai Jaijee Modi had begun the construction of a fire temple (Atash Behram) in the memory of her late husband Dadabhai Nusserwanji Modi. A fire sparked by lightning is one of the necessary ingredients in the construction of a fire temple and the Zoroastrians of Surat were on the lookout for such a fire. Calcutta had also received this message. On 4 May 1823, Navroji Sorabji Umrigar (Bengalee) and his friends were relaxing in the evening at the bungalow of Rustomji Cowasji Banaji in the Cotton Ginning & Pressing factory, situated on the west bank of the Hooghly. Suddenly the sky became overcast and there was thunder and lightning. A bolt of lightning set a nearby banana tree on fire. Thanking God for this fire, Navroji took a branch of the smouldering tree into the house and kept the fire going by heaping incense and sandalwood on it. The night was spent in keeping the fire alive and offering prayers with great veneration and devotion. The next morning the fire was taken to the house of Navroji Sorabji Umrigar (Bengalee), where a special place was kept aside for Parsis to offer prayers to it with constant offering of sandalwood and incense. The 'fire' was then sent to Bombay by a ship called *Mumbai Kaptan*, in the care of two Zoroastrians with strict instructions to keep the fire alive. From Bombay, this fire, ignited by a bolt of lightning, was sent to Surat. An account of this episode appeared in the *Mumbai Samachar* on 15 May 1823 under the signature of Navroji Sorabji Umrigar, Rustomji Cowasji Banaji, Dorabji Behramji Bengali, Navrojee Jamshedjee, Bomanjee Ratanjee and Meherwanji Limjibhai Billimoria.

THE BANAJI FAMILY IN CALCUTTA

In 1837 Calcutta was one of the dirtiest cities in the world. Rustomji Cowasji Banaji played a major role in the making of the modern city of Calcutta. He was the first Parsi to bring his entire family including women and children to the city. The widespread publicity of this fact implies that it was a unique event. Rustomji was very modern in his outlook. This was reflected in his religious views as well when he built the Banaji Atash Adaran in Calcutta in 1839. It was meant for both sects of Zoroastrians, Shahanshais and Kadimis.

The history of the Banaji family in Calcutta begins in the year 1750. Banaji Limji was born in Bhagradandi near Surat. When the British shifted their operations from Surat to Bombay, he came to Bombay in 1690. He started his own trading business in opium and silk with China, Burma, Siam and some other countries. Each voyage would take six to twelve months.

Dadabhai Behramji, grandson of Banaji Limji, was the first Parsi to come to Calcutta in 1767. When John Cartier was appointed Governor of Bengal, he persuaded his friend Dadabhai to follow him to Calcutta.

Rustomji Cowasji Banaji was the nephew of Dadabhai Behramji. In Bengal, he was affectionately called 'Rustomji Babu'. He was born in Bombay in 1792 and came to Calcutta in 1812. He made two voyages to China and then in 1817 he made Calcutta his home. In 1821 he started his own business in the name of 'Rustomji Cowasji'.

Dwarkanath Tagore

Rustomji Cowasji

Photo courtesy: Saga of Security: Story of Indian Life Insurance

He was the first Indian to venture into a partnership with the British. His partnership with Robert Turner was called 'Rustomji Turner & Company of Calcutta'.

Rustomji was a close friend of Dwarkanath Tagore, the grandfather of Rabindranath Tagore. Dwarkanath Tagore also founded a company in 1834 called Carr, Tagore & Company.

The Government Gazette of 3 April 1828 published a list of persons eligible for special jurors in the Supreme Court of Calcutta, with the necessary qualification. Rustomji was described in it as a merchant owning properties worth two lakhs of rupees.

Raja Rammohan Roy emphasised that the salvation of India lay in its industrial development. Rustomji Cowasji and Dwarkanath Tagore tried to realise the ideas preached by the Raja.

Insurance

Rustomji was passionately involved in the insurance business. The *Calcutta Monthly Journal* 1835 states:

> The committee of insurance offices have deputed Mr WM Carr and Rustomji Cowasji to receive and distribute the funds, and they paid the amount of salvage on 25th September without waiting for the bill of lading etc. which was remitted from China to the Agent of Captain Hawkins, being delivered into their possession.

He was a member of the Union Insurance Company England and had large financial partnerships in the English Insurance Company, The Laudible Societies, The Sun Life Office, The Oriental Insurance Company, The Indian Laudible & Mutual Insurance Company.

Banking

In July 1834, Rustomji was elected Director of The Union Bank. In the *British Friend of India* magazine dated 21 July 1842 we find a reference to Rustomji: 'Rustomjee gave up the post of Director in favour of his son Maneckji Rustomji. Rustomji remained the biggest shareholder in the bank.' Owing to the scheming of interested parties, including its European directors, the bank finally collapsed in 1848. In those days, when the banking system was in its infancy, shareholders were held responsible for a bank's failure. Creditors could sue any and every shareholder to realise their dues. Rustomji lost his entire fortune trying to settle the creditors' claims. Once a merchant prince, he was reduced to a beggar on the streets after the crash.

Shipping

Shipbuilding was a lucrative business in the early nineteenth century. Rustomji Cowasji started the Docking Company on 16 January 1837. He purchased the Kidderpore Docks from the estate of the late James Kedd at Rs 2,51,000 and Salkia Docks from M/S Kerry & Company at Rs 2,00,000.

The *British Friend of India* (26 October 1843) wrote:

> The 13th half yearly meeting of the Docking Company was held at the office of the Secretary, Rustomji Cowasji Esqr. To all appearances, it was the most flourishing company in Calcutta. It works with a capital of about rupees 6 lakhs and pays its secretaries, as it is said, 2000 rupees a month and is yet able to divide a profit of 16%.

Rustomji Cowasji was also a prominent ship owner in those days. Rustomji Cowasji & Company was heavily into shipbuilding. It owned about forty ships. They carried out trade between Calcutta, Madras, Ceylon, Bombay, Singapore, China and Melbourne. The ship-launching ceremony was reported in contemporary newspapers. The *British Friend of India* (13 December 1839) noted:

> The 'Rustomji Cowasji' which was launched at Kidderpore in July last, has established a character for sailing, which few even of the clippers; have maintained. She arrived in Macao on the 5th of October, after a passage of only 11 days, from Singapore. She has beaten the Sir Edward Ryan, the best of the clippers, six days in the passage from Singapore.

Half of Rustomji's ships were chartered by the British Government 1839 onwards for war purposes for Rs 11,500 a month. *The Golconda*, one of Rustomji's ships, was destroyed in the China War. Some of his ships also carried mail to different countries and some were hired for sending Indian labourers to the Mauritius Islands.

Rustomji Banaji had vast trading interests in China and one of the principal commodities traded was opium. The ships were called Opium Clippers. In 1839 the Chinese government forbade all trade in opium and ordered all opium traders in China to surrender their entire stock of opium lying in Chinese ports. The Chinese army took over the offices of the European and Parsi traders and seized all the opium. The traders were arrested. Later, due to the efforts of the British Ambassador to China, they were all released. It was estimated that opium worth rupees three crores was seized. This was a great loss for all the traders.

Meanwhile, the route to the west via the Suez Canal was discovered and Rustomji Cowasji, Dwarkanath Tagore, Motilal Seal, Ram Comul Sen and nine Europeans started a company called Percursor Scheme Committee to carry mail between the Suez and Calcutta.

The Indian General Steam Navigation Company with Rustomji Cowasji, the only Indian, on its board was started in 1844 to formulate an inland steam navigation system.

Social Reformer

As a social reformer, his public activities in social, political and intellectual spheres had far-reaching effects.

In 1838 Rustomji brought his entire family to Calcutta by sea. This extraordinary event was widely reported in the newspapers. The *Bombay Gazette* of 16 July 1838 wrote:

> Our Parsi friends, who have for so long been foremost among the natives of this country in everything connected with commercial enterprise, are now about to set an example in what may at first sight be considered a purely domestic matter but which will in all probability in its ulterior results, from throwing aside the trammels of ancient prejudices, mean the production of singular changes. The lady of Rustomji Cowasji, the distinguished and liberal minded merchant of Calcutta, is about to sail from Bombay for that Port in a few days, accompanied by the wife of his son, and a cortege of female attendants. To those who remember that but a few years ago, no Parsi female of respectability would proceed

> even to the Deccan. The contemplated trip of these fair villagers will afford such food for application upon the rapid change which the march of opinion has affected.

Samachar Darpan reported on 18 August 1838:

> We are happy to hear that the lady of our worthy citizen Rustomji Cowasji Esqr., has just arrived by sea from Bombay. The ladies among the Parsis have the same aversion to going on board ships which the Hindu and Mohommedan ladies feel. This, therefore, is the first instance in which the tyranny of custom has been overcome. We think that Rustomjee deserves great credit for the boldness with which he has broken through this pernicious custom.

He provided every opportunity to the women of his family to relinquish the purdah: 'He, breaking through the restraints usual among his countrymen, did not hesitate to introduce the ladies of his family to his guests, among whom the Governor General has more than once been present' (*The Englishman*, 19 April 1852).

Social Service

Rustomji Cowasji was a committed social worker and encouraged education. Reproduced below are some of the charitable acts he was involved in.

The Sambad Baskar of 7 April 1846 wrote:

> We cannot say too much of the merits of Rustomji Cowasji. The canal on the other side of Bahir Road (the upper Circular Road) which owes its existence to his munificence, is now adorning the city. Besides, he has done many good works, especially, he has

> now awarded gold medals to his students of the Medical College. Everyone will therefore congratulate him on this noble action of his.

In memory of Dwarkanath Tagore, the Dwarkanath Tagore Endowment Fund was opened in 1846 to provide cultural and technical education to a fixed number of boys in the University College of London. Rustomji Cowasji was a trustee of this fund.

The Agricultural and Horticultural Society was formed by Rev. William Carey in the early nineteenth century. Rustomji contributed liberally to the society. He gave financial aid to build Metcalfe Hall, the society's permanent abode.

Rustomji was very liberal with his wealth. *The Englishman* reported on 10 April 1852: 'Rustomji was extremely liberal while he had the means and there must have been many yet living who have felt his kindness when it was of the utmost value to them.'

According to the *Modern Review*, July 1833, Rustomji's contribution to the improvement of Calcutta cannot be over estimated. Tiled huts, streets, tanks, drainage, hospitals, ferry system bear testimony to his love of the city. The District Charitable Society of Calcutta (1837) supports this assertion.

Calcutta had a notorious reputation for disease, filth and unsanitary conditions about 200 years ago. Fever and cholera were rampant. Rustomji established the first Fever Hospital in the city. Fire broke out in April and May 1837 and hundreds of huts were burnt to ashes rendering people homeless. Rustomji realised that lack of water and the straw-thatched roofs were the main reason for the fire.

Rustomji Cowasji Banaji in his report in the first sub-committee established to investigate the causes of and suggest remedies for fire outbreaks, noted:

> Having been present at several of the fires that have devastated the city, I beg to lay before the meeting a statement of facts that came under my personal observation. During the great fire that extended all along the Upper Circular Road, I particularly noticed the scarcity of water. There being few if any, tanks in the vicinity.

Therefore he recommended that a line of deep, large tanks should be immediately dug, at convenient distances all along Upper Circular Road, where water was scarcer than any other part of the town.

> The ground might now be purchased at moderate prices before the proprietors have time to erect new huts. I think the government ought to bear the expenses, but as an inducement for them to come forward, I will undertake if government will buy the ground, to excavate at my own expense four large tanks between Boitaconnah, Mirzapore and Manicktallah and I am sure that many rich landholders will readily do as much or more in other parts of the town.

In addition, he had many tanks excavated on his own land at his own personal expense.

Straw huts were one of the primary causes of fire. Bombay and Madras had already introduced tiled huts. Seeing this, Rustomji argued for tiled huts in Calcutta as well. Finally a committee with Rustomji and Dwarkanath Tagore was formed to fund people to build tiled huts.

Another aspect of life in Calcutta that attracted Rustomji's attention was the ferry system. In those days the ferry system was flawed. There were no fixed ghats to land or to moor the boats on, which were thus often sunk by the boatmen and the belongings of passengers robbed. Rustomji suggested that the ghats should be numbered and registered and the name of the owner, together with the number of passengers the boat was permitted to carry, should be painted in legible characters on a conspicuous part of the boat. Large ferries were stringently monitored, the boats were classified, the rate of hire was fixed, and both boats and boatmen were to be examined as to their efficiency every month.

Rustomji Cowasji died on 16 April 1852. Readers of both English and vernacular newspapers were notified about his death. *The Englishman* (19 April 1852), *British Friend of India* and *The Statesman* were some of the newspapers and magazines that carried news of his demise. Extracts from his obituary that appeared in *The Englishman* (19 April 1852) have already been quoted. It deserves to be quoted in its entirety:

> Rustomji has resided about 33 years in Calcutta and for a greater part of that time carried on a very extensive business as a merchant and a ship owner, and for his activity and enterprise, was well known to men of business all over the East. During his prosperity he sought the European society and breaking through the restraints usual among his countrymen, did not hesitate to introduce the ladies of his family to his guests, among whom the Governor General has more than once been present. When what is called a commercial crisis visited Calcutta, Rustomji shared in the misfortune of his neighbours and lost nearly all that he had been working for during a long and laborious life. He has since that time lived in a very retired manner, and as his health also declined, he utterly withdrew in a great measure from business. The cause of his death is stated to have been disease of heart, which at his advanced age could not be expected to have other than a fatal termination. Rustomji was extremely liberal while he had the means and there must be many yet living who have felt his kindness when it was of the utmost value to them.

Four geographical landmarks bearing his name still exist in Calcutta and Cossipore: Rustomjee Street near Ballygunge Phari; Parsi Bagan, the site of his bungalow on Upper Circular Road; Rustomjee Ghat in Cossipore; and Rustomjee Parsi Road in the same neighbourhood.

Rustomji built a fire temple at his own expense at one of his properties in Calcutta. The Atash Adaran was consecrated on 16 September 1839. Dastur Khurshed Dastur Bejon came from Bombay to Calcutta on foot carrying the 'holy *alaat*' which was required for the consecration ceremony attended by all the Parsis of Calcutta. After the *Jashan*, he announced that the religious rites of both the Kadimi and Shahanshai sects will be performed in this *dar-e-meher* and he also created a separate estate for the permanent upkeep of the *dar-e-meher* with the trust remaining in his control and, after his death, in the control of his heirs in perpetuity. Next to the *dar-e-meher*, a separate block was built which had facilities for *ghambars* (community feasts) and also a furnished house with utensils for Parsi travellers.

The plaque on the Atash Adaran reads:

> *In the name of Dadgar Dadar Ahuramazda*
> *This Atash Adaran was built by Seth Rustomji Cowasji Banaji for the use of Zarthostis of Calcutta and to perform prayers and religious rites according to the tenets of the Mazdayasni religion and was consecrated in the third year of the reign of Queen Victoria of England, roz 17 Sarosh, Mah I Farvandin, Kadimi year 1209 Y.Z.*
> *16th September 1839, Monday*

Maneckji Rustomji Banaji was the son of Rustomji Cowasji Banaji. He was well respected in government circles and was very popular within and outside the community.

Hirjibhai Maneckji Rustomji Banaji

Maneckji Rustomji Banaji (1815-1891)

Maneckji was a director of National Bank of India and was on the board of several companies. In 1870, the Shah of Persia appointed him the first Counsel to look after his interest in India in the British Government circles.

In 1874, he was the first Indian to be appointed Sheriff of Calcutta. He also served as a Justice of Peace. He was an Honorary Magistrate and a Commissioner of the Calcutta Municipality. He died in 1891. In his memory an endowment for the prize of a gold medal was made in Calcutta University. In 1898 his portrait was installed in Town Hall and at that function, he was extolled as a cheerful and philanthropic merchant. Unveiling his portrait, the Governor of Bengal, Sir Alexander Mackenzie, said:

> There was no man in all Calcutta more respected and esteemed by every section of the community, European and native. In all his public offices he did his duty in a quiet, unobtrusive unostentatious way and never dreamt of making office serve him. In this way he won for himself a reputation and position which was in its way unique. To men of the present generation he was a living link with the past. He had seen 15 Governor Generals come and go and known them all, and his memory had stored up a wealth of experience such as no other man in Calcutta could pretend to. This experience and hoarded wisdom he devoted to the cause of peace and goodwill, and he inherited in the love and respect of every class of the community that blessing which is the sure reward of the peace-maker under whatever religions persuasion he may be found.

The Trust Deed of the Calcutta Zoroastrian Community's Religious & Charity Funds was formulated in 1864 under his leadership and he served as one of its first three trustees for twenty-seven long years (1864-1891). In his memory, the Parsi Anjuman of Calcutta collected funds and built the Maneckji Rustomji Dharamsala in Bow Street.

Maneckji's son, ***Hirjibhai Maneckji Rustomji Banaji***, was also a Counsel for Persia, a Sheriff of Calcutta and a fellow of Calcutta University. The British awarded him the Companion of the Indian Empire. He was a trustee of the Calcutta Zoroastrian Community's Religious & Charity Funds for many years.

Hirjibhai had two sons: Rustomji and Curshedji. Rustomji served as an Honorary Presidency Magistrate of Calcutta, Councillor of the Municipal Corporation and as a member of several public institutions. Curshedji served as a trustee of the Calcutta Zoroastrian Community's Religious & Charity Funds, he was an Honorary Presidency Magistrate and a visitor of the Alipore

Central Jail. He was also the founder of the Parsee Zoroastrian Association of Calcutta.

Centenary Celebrations of the Seth Rustomji Cowasji Banaji Atash Adaran in 1939: A report by Jaloo Navel Kanga

13th August 1939 will remain a red letter day in the history of the Parsis of Calcutta. On that auspicious day, the Centenary of the Seth Rustomji Cowasji Banaji Atash Adaran was celebrated by the entire Parsi community of Calcutta with great joy and enthusiasm.

As the day dawned, the trustees of the holy fire temple offered a sandalwood machi to the fire in havan gah. At 8.30 in the morning a thanksgiving Jashan ceremony was performed in which a large number of men, women and children participated. The mobed sahebs of the second fire temple in Calcutta, Late Ervad DB Mehta's Atash Adaran took part in the actual ceremony. After the Jashan, the senior trustees of the Adaran and Seth Khurshedji Hirjibhai Maneckji Rustomji Banaji offered sandalwood and prayers to the fire and gave tokens of appreciation to the priests.

In the afternoon at 3 pm in Ujiran gah, a machi was offered on behalf of the entire community. Both these machis were put up on the fire by the senior priest Ervad Kaikhushroo Rustomji Kohin. At 4 pm another Jashan was performed on behalf of the Anjuman and the presence of men, women and children who had come to attend the ceremony lent an air of festivity to Ezra Street. After the Jashan, a solemn and dignified meeting was held in the ornate shamiana in the compound under the chairmanship of Seth Edalji Olpadvala, the senior trustee of the Anjuman Charity Funds. The stage was occupied by the senior trustee of the Adaran, Seth Khurshedji HM Rustomji Banaji, Trustees of the Anjuman Seth Edalji S Olpadvala and Seth Jamshedji B Dastoor, the priests of both the fire temples and members of the reception committee. After the inaugural speeches, the oldest Parsi resident of Calcutta, Seth Meherwanji Cowasji Gora, described the history of the illustrious Banaji family and read out the address of felicitation on behalf of the Calcutta Parsi Anjuman. This address, printed on silk and worked in silver and gold thread, was encased in a silver casket and presented to Seth Khurshedji HM Banaji with a shawl. On behalf of the Anjuman, shawls were presented also to Seth Manekji Khurshedji and Seth Faramji Khurshjedji. Thereafter, Seth Jamshedji B. Dastoor presented a shawl to Seth Khurshedji, recalling the fact that his (Jamshedji's) maternal grandfather Dastoor Khurshed Dastoor Bejon and his revered father Bejonji had brought the sacred alaat on foot from Bombay one hundred years ago for the consecration of this holy fire temple. Shawls were also presented by Seth Edalji S. Olpadvala and Seth Meherwanji Cowasji Gora. Seth Khurshedji in expressing his grateful thanks to the community said that this Atash Adaran has been serving all the religious needs of the local Parsis for the past hundred years and expressed a hope and a prayer that it will continue to do so for many centuries to come.

At this function, the sons of Seth Hormasji Edalji Bilimoria were thanked for the gifts of beautiful carpets for use in the Atash Adaran. A shawl was presented to Seth Ardeshir Dinshah Vevalvala in appreciation of his services in connection with the repairs and maintenance of the buildings of the Atash Adaran. Other recipients of the shawls were the trustees of the Anjuman Charity Funds, Seth Edalji S Olpadvala and Seth Jamshedji B Dastoor. Thanks were given to Seth Jehangirji J Modi for his strenuous efforts in collecting funds for the centenary celebrations. The editor of *Navroz,* Seth Edalji N Kanga, said that the Calcutta Parsis will cherish the memory of this happy and auspicious day for many years and he congratulated all the members of the community for enthusiastically taking part in the celebrations.

A well-organised community dinner followed at The Clem Brown Institute. About a thousand Parsis participated in it and it was the first time in the history of Parsis of Calcutta that such a large number sat down to dinner together. The boy scouts, under the leadership of scout master Mr Ardeshir K Batlivala, rendered praiseworthy services.

The premises of the Adaran were decorated with electric lights and flowers and all families observed the day as a festival. Parsi school children in English and Gujarati schools were given the day off to enable them to participate in the festivities.

(*Navroz*, 26 August 1939)

EARLY PARSIS OF CALCUTTA
(1830 ONWARDS)

After China banned the opium trade, Parsis diversified into the cotton and jute-manufacturing industry. This was also the time of the great Reform in the Zoroastrian religion. Many Hindu customs had entered into the religion and the Avestan scholars called for a 'return to the Gathas*'. In addition, Christian missionaries dubbed the teachings of Zoroaster as nature worship and accused the faith of dualism. The religious scholars had recently translated the* Gathas *and knew that Zoroastrianism was a monotheistic religion meant for all mankind. It was a time of growth and churn and, despite the context of the size of the community, Parsis stood out for their pioneering instincts, their justice and philanthropy as well as their endeavour to go back to their roots.*

Dorabjee Behramjee Bengali came to Calcutta and made a name for himself as a businessman. He was popular with Bengali merchants who called him Dorabjee Babu. He was involved in trade with China and had his own ship. In later years, he suffered great losses and had to wind up his business. He died in 1838 at the age of sixty-eight.

Meherwanji Limji Billimoria arrived in Calcutta around 1820-1822 and started his own business as a commission agent. In 1833 he built a 'pucca' bridge on the road leading to the Tower of Silence in his native place of Billimoria in Gujarat. In those days, Parsis had to pay an annual tribute of Rs 51 to the Government of Gaekwad of

Baroda. He bought a large orchard in Parol village near Amalsad and donated it to the Parsi Anjuman there, so that the tribute could be paid out of its proceeds.

Dhunjibhai Rustomji Wadia was the younger son of the well-known Bombay shipbuilder, Rustomji Maneckji Lovji. After training under his father, he came to Calcutta in 1837 and joined Rustomji Cowasji Banaji's Calcutta Docking Company, as a master builder at the company's Kidderpore Docks. He built many ships and some of them were used to carry cargo during the wars in China (1840-1841).

Framji Pestonji Nalladaroo was the first High Priest of Banaji Agiari. He came all the way from Surat by bullock cart. He served at the Agiari for five years and then started his own business. He was a scholar of the Pahlavi language and a Persian teacher in the Jamshedji Jeejeebhoy Baronet School in Surat. After serving as Head Priest in the Agiari, he started his own business, FN Nalladaroo & Co., in 1870 with the assistance of his sons, Byramji and Navroji, trading with China. Byramji would look after the Calcutta business and Navroji mostly travelled between China and India. This company then started trading with Japan, Italy and Czechoslovakia.

Munchershaw Buttiwala

Byramji Nalladaroo

Navroji and Byramji Nalladaroo

The Calcutta Parsi Club at the Maidan was started in 1908 by two brothers – Navroji and Byramji Nalladaroo.

Navroji was the first Parsi to be born in Calcutta and also the first Parsi to start playing tennis. In those days only Europeans played this game. Navroji was also a homeopathic doctor ('pani ka doctor').

Five stalwarts of those days, Munchershaw Buttiwala, Byramji Nalladaroo, Navroji Nalladaroo, Hormasjee Kandawalla and Keki Spencer, got together and founded The Calcutta Parsee Club (name later changed to Calcutta Parsi Club) on 4 November 1908.

Khurshedji Bomanji Motabhai was a resident of Calcutta in the middle of the nineteenth century. In 1845 several merchants from the Hindu, Marwari and other communities started an agitation in Calcutta for the establishment of a society for the prevention of cruelty to animals. Khurshedji Bomanji Motabhai made a petition to the British Government on 24 October 1845 to enact a law to that effect. He wrote several articles in the local newspapers, such as *Bengal Harkara* and *Calcutta Star,* to keep this movement alive. Finally, the Society for Prevention of Cruelty to Animals was founded in Calcutta and Bombay.

Meherwanji Mehta, the father of Sir Phirozeshah Mehta, came to Calcutta in 1845 as a representative of Cama & Company and stayed in Calcutta for some time.

Khurshedji Rustomji Cama, the well-known scholar and religious teacher, came to Calcutta in 1849 and achieved fame as the first public speaker in Calcutta, on religious and social subjects.

In his school days, Cama had been persuaded by Dr John Wilson to attend services at St Thomas' Cathedral. Later, he would attend small discussion groups on the Christian religion. The missionaries

Phirozeshah Mehta

Pioneer Parsi Zend and Avestic Scholars – Mr. K.R. Kama and his Pupils

Sitting, left to right: (1) Ervud Tehmurus Dinshaw Anklesaria, 1840-1903; (2) Ervud Sheriarji Dadabhoy Bharucha, 1843-1915; (3) Mr. Khurshedji Rustomji Kama, 1831-1909; (4) Ervud Kavasji Edulji Kanga, 1839-1904; (5) Ervud Edulji Kershapji Antia, 1842-1913.

Standing: (1) Ervud Jamsetji Dadabhoy Nadirshaw; 1846-1913 (2) Ervud Khurshedji Minocherji Kateli, 1826-1902.

dubbed the teachings of Zoroaster nature worship and accused Zoroastrians of dualism. His mother got to hear of this, rebutted this and made him promise not to go to such meetings in the future.

Luckily for Cama, he travelled to England with Dadabhai Naoroji, who belonged to the Bhuggasarth priest family of Navsari, and he explained to Cama the tenets of the Zoroastrian religion and that it was a monotheistic religion.

On his return to Bombay, Khurshedji started teaching the religion. His first student was Ervad Sheriarji Dadabhoy Bharucha. Lawrence Mills, Jackson and Martin Haug first inspired KR Cama (who started his business life in Calcutta) and he set up the school for *Zend* & *Avesta* studies.

Many eminent scholars on the *Avesta* were his students: Dastur Peshotan Sanjana, Ervad Kavasji Edulji Kanga, Sir Jeevanji Jamshedji Modi, Dastur MN Dhalla, Tehmuras Anklesaria and Behrampore Anklesaria. They were selected for the Expert Committee on Religion in 1908 in the Petit Vs Jeejeebhoy case. The committee expressed the view that conversion was a tenet of the Zoroastrian religion.

Dadabhai Naoroji

Dadabhai Naoroji started the Religious Reform Movement in 1855 calling for the return to the *Gathas* to remove the Hindu customs that had entered their religion. He maintained that the Zoroastrian religion was not meant for a small tribe but a monotheistic religion meant for all mankind. He launched the magazine *Raast Goftar* or the 'Truth Teller' to clarify Zoroastrian concepts and promote Parsi social reform. He also founded the Rahnumae Mazdayasne

Sabha (Guides on the Mazdayasni Path) to restore the Zoroastrian religion to its original purity and simplicity.

Dadabhai Naoroji was a close family friend of our RD Mehta who built the second Agiari in Calcutta and when in Calcutta would stay at the Mehta residence.

Ervad Dhanjishah Nusserwanji Nalladaroo was the son of Framji Nusserwanji. He served as a priest of the Banaji Atash Behram for seven years. He was fond of music and could play the concertina and other instruments. He discovered that there was no guide to German concertina and accordion for Bengali music students. He studied Bengali and with the help of his music teacher, Babu Pannalal Roy, wrote the book *German Concertina Accordion Shika* and published it in 1896. This is the only book published in Bengali by a Parsi in Calcutta.

Cowasji Pestonji Gora came to Calcutta around 1860. He had large trading interests in China. He was close friends with many British residents in Calcutta. He was one of the first trustees of the Calcutta Zoroastrian Community's Religious & Charity Fund where he served from 1864-1868. He died at the age of seventy-one in 1899 on roz 29 Marespand, Mah 4 Tir, year 1268 y.z., corresponding to 11 January 1899. His son K Cowasji Gora was an architect who helped in the construction of New Market.

Framji Mancherji Bumlakhau was born in Navsari in 1839. He had lost his father at an early age and his childhood was spent in poverty. During the Indian Mutiny of 1857 he was arrested but Lord Roberts befriended him and he was released and returned to Navsari. His father had served as a caretaker for Sir Jamshedjee Jeejeebhoy when he was a baby. This prompted him to give Framji Bumlakhau Rs 3,000. Framji Bumlakhau used this money to come to Calcutta,

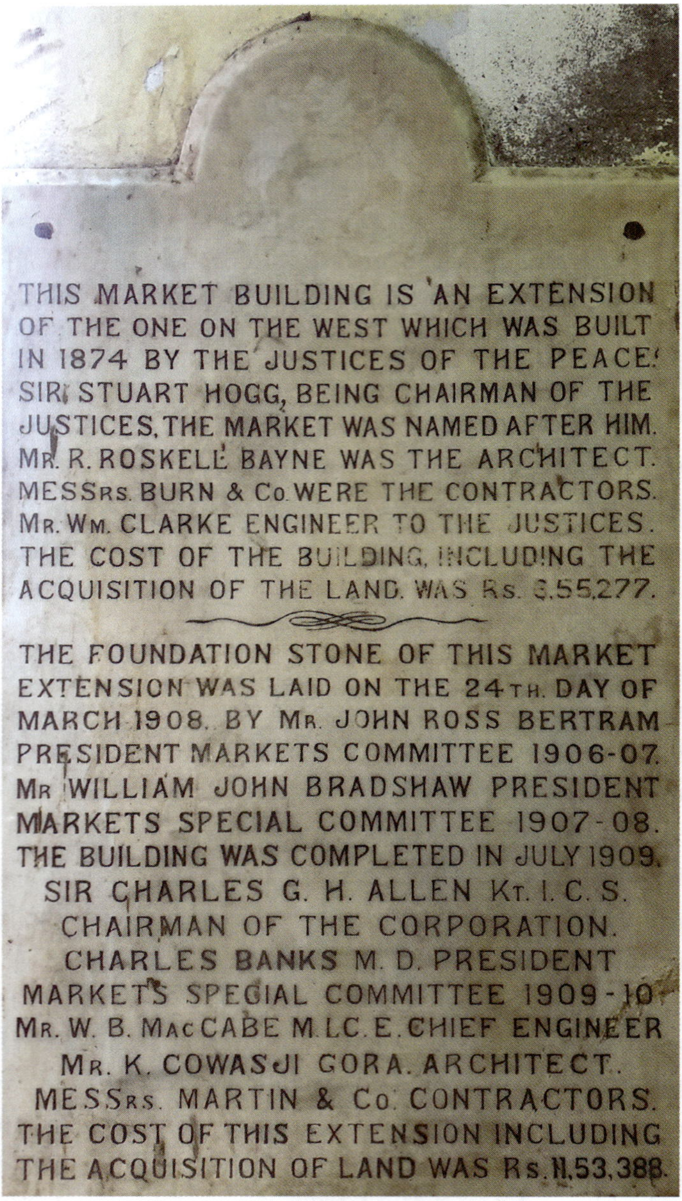

Plaque at New Market dated 24 March 1908:
'Mr K. Cowasji Gora – Architect'
Photo courtesy: Samudrika Armstead

Framji Mancherji Bumlakhau, an old-time prominent merchant of Calcutta

travelling the entire distance by horse carriage (*ekka*), to try his luck in partnership with his close friend Nusserwanji Bankwala, manager of Amritsar Bank. Framji sent goods from Calcutta to Nusserwanji in Punjab. His very first transaction in Tennants Beer of Watson Green & Company earned him considerable profit. He also received several railway contracts and he developed a large business with Punjab. Framji opened the first Parsi shop in Darjeeling.

During the famine of 1900-1902 Framji constructed a big tank in Muzaffarpur and a big well in Samastipur, and helped the famine-struck people with food, clothing and money. Besides, he also built tanks and wells in his hometown Navsari, in Daman and Bhimpore. In Navsari, in memory of Jamshedjee Jeejeebhoy, he donated land for a school. Another Parsi from Calcutta, Meherwanji Mehta, built the school building and the boundary wall.

In 1882, the Maharaja Sayajirao Gaekwad of Baroda and the Maharani Saheba came to Calcutta with a retinue of 700 people. Framji made all the arrangements with pomp and ceremony and won the admiration and respect of the Maharaja. In appreciation of his services, the Maharaja presented him with a gold watch studded with diamonds, bearing his personal monogram, a gold watch and chain, a diamond ring and a cash gift of Rs 2,500. Later, at Framji's son's wedding, the Maharaja sent royal gifts consisting of four pairs of brocade shawls, both of fine silk, and twenty-one gold *mohors*.

Framji died in 1934.

Edulji Pestonji Guzdar came from Gandevi to Calcutta in 1867. The journey took him three months as he came by bullock cart. He started trading with China in rice. In 1880 he started a jute baling press in Ghusury, Howrah. In 1893 he started the Victoria Cotton Mills.

He served as a trustee of the Calcutta Zoroastrian Community's Religious & Charity Funds, from 1882-1914. He formed a partnership with Jeevanlal Motichand for the manufacture of aluminium utensils and later established a glass factory called Victoria Glass Works.

Mohtabhai Cooverji Guzdar

Mohtabhai Cooverji Guzdar, Pestonji's nephew, grew up in Calcutta and joined his uncle's business. He was a patron of the Calcutta Parsi Club. He served as a Secretary of the Calcutta Parsi Amateur Dramatic Club for thirty-two years till his death in 1949. He also served as a trustee of the Calcutta Zoroastrian Community's Religious & Charity Funds from 1938-1949.

JAMSETJEE FRAMJEE MADON

Jamsetjee Framjee Madon was one of the pioneers of Indian cinema. He owned over 120 cinema halls at one time. Jamsetjee was very modern in his outlook and a reformist in his religious views. He was one of the first trustees of the Late Ervad D.B. Mehta's Zoroastrian Anjuman Atash Adaran and was a supporter of the young Bella, to whom he left Rs 5,000 in his will to help her in her legal case.

Jamsetjee Framjee Madon was born on 27 April 1856 in a very poor family in Bombay. The family being truly indigent, he had to seek employment at the tender age of twelve as a scene-shifter in the dramatic company of Cooverji Ratanji Nazir, at a salary of Rs 4 per month. The young lad got enamoured of the stage, copying the roles of the heroes and heroines of the plays and later playing small roles on stage. Since he had a good voice, he could act the part of a courtesan and became quite popular.

He then joined Elphinstone Natak Company which toured the country and in 1875, on an auspicious day, he came to Calcutta with this touring company. Some time later he took over this company in partnership with a few others. This company prospered, thanks to his experience, far-sightedness and hard work, and made Calcutta its permanent home. Simultaneously he started dealing in auctioned goods and in 1885 started another business as wines and provision merchant at 5, Dharamtalla Street. His honesty, perseverance and gentle nature soon attracted important Indian customers and the shop became extremely popular among government officers and

Jamsetjee Framjee Madon, the Merchant Prince of Calcutta

Englishmen. There were seven branches of this store including those at Calcutta, Darjeeling, Lucknow and Delhi.

In 1903, at the time of the British invasion of Tibet, Jamsetjee opened food and provision stores all the way from Siliguri to Chumbi and assisted the armed forces in supplying food and provision to soldiers even at great personal risk. The British officers greatly appreciated Madon's fortitude and bravery as a result of which Jamsetjee was given a large contract of supplying the army during the wars in Kabul. He carried out his work at great risk and in significantly difficult circumstances, to the utmost satisfaction of the military officers. In appreciation of these services, the British Government awarded him the Order of the British Empire in 1918.

On 30 March 1919, the Calcutta Parsis felicitated Jamsetjee at a function under the chairmanship of the trustee of the Anjuman, Seth Edulji Pestonji Guzdar. Madon Seth was congratulated on obtaining the Order of the British Empire and praised for his simple life, gentle nature, honesty and kindness and for his munificence towards the poor.

Shehen-Shaw Jehangir. *A play with music in 1927. Price 1 anna a ticket*

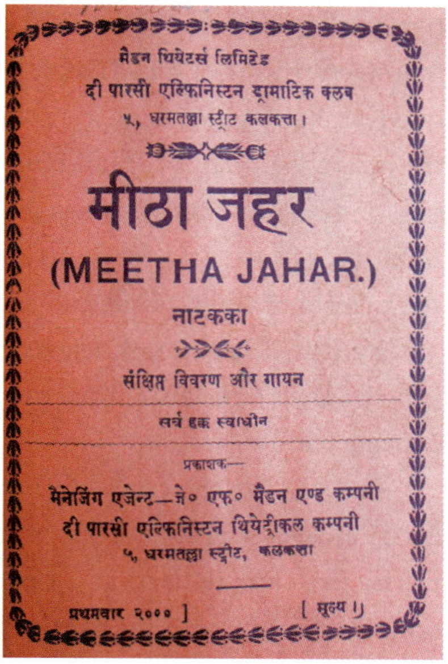

Madon Theatre Limited, Parsi Elphinstone Theatrical Company, 5 Dharamtalla Street. Advertisement for Meetha Jahar *in 1917*

Seth Jamsetjee, like the other Parsi elders of the community, had a generous nature and was always anxious to assist the needy. Having grown up in poverty he felt for the poor and gave employment to many poor Parsi youngsters in his cinemas and shops. He was thus responsible for the livelihood of a large number of Parsi families. Many of his charities were done secretly and it can be truly said of him that his left hand was not aware of what his right hand gave away. It was estimated that such secret handouts averaged Rs 5,000 every month. This help was not restricted to Parsis exclusively; all the needy benefitted from his charity, irrespective of caste or creed. Many institutions of public welfare owed their existence and prosperity to him.

In 1907 Seth Jamsetjee took up the mission of building a second Tower of Silence in Calcutta. Starting a subscription list with his personal donation of Rs 5,000, he went from house to house and managed to collect a lakh of rupees from the Calcutta Parsis. It was due to his influence that the municipality gave a grant of Rs 27,000 towards the purchase of land for this second Tower of Silence, and he personally bore the expenses of Rs 20,000 towards building it. Seth Madon's efforts and far-sightedness resulted in bringing together the priests of the Kadimi and Shahanshai sections for the first time in Calcutta. The Kadimi priests performed the religious rites at the time of the foundation and the Shahanshai priests performed the consecration rites.

In 1912, at the time of the building of the Mehta fire temple, Seth Jamsetjee provided his devoted services. The building attached to the fire temple used as a residence for the priests was built and donated by him and his family to the Atash Adaran. He presented several chandeliers, lamps and carpets for the main prayer hall and also many tables, chairs, large cooking utensils for general use. This generous-hearted Parsi also had the foresight to start funds with initial personal donations to take care of the future maintenance of the Atash Adaran.

Seth Jamsetjee was deeply sympathetic towards the poor Parsi families in Calcutta. In Dharamtalla Street he built Khorshed Madan Mansion at an expense of Rs 1,10,176 in memory of his beloved daughter, Mrs Khorshed Rustomji Maneckji Mehta, who had died on 14 January 1920 during the lifetime of her parents. Seth Jamsetjee donated this house to the Anjuman on the understanding that the flats be rented out to the poor and middle-class Parsi families of Calcutta at a low rent. Further he set aside a sizeable fund for the maintenance of this building.

He also secured the land for the 'aramgah' for the Parsis in Darjeeling and donated funds towards its maintenance. On several occasions he gave donations to the Anjuman on behalf of his friends and relations. Seth Jamsetjee organised several 'benefit nights' in many of his cinema houses to collect funds for charities for Parsis as well as other communities.

In 1923, the British Government honoured him with the award of Commander of the Order of the British Empire in recognition of his many cosmopolitan charities.

About twenty years prior to the advent of cinema on a commercial basis in India, Seth Jamsetjee experimented with this new media and perfected it for public viewing. He was truly a pioneer of the cinema industry in India.

The young lad of twelve, who started his career as a scene-shifter at a salary of Rs 4 per month, aided by some lucky turn of events and greatly due to his own inherent ability, perseverance and hard labour, became, in the evening of his life, the owner of a hundred cinema houses in India. Seth Jamsetjee's life is a shining example of Parsi adventure and philanthropy. Upon his death which took place in Calcutta on roz 22 Govad, Mah 10 Dae, Year 1292 y.z., corresponding to 28 June 1923, Calcutta lost a true benefactor of the poor.

Seth Jamsetjee's wife Bai Pirojbai was a very kind-hearted, gentle and religious lady. She always assisted her husband in all his charities and gave donations from her personal funds. She died in 1938, leaving behind a large family.

Seth Jamsetjee's eldest son Burjorji served as a trustee of the Anjuman Atash Adaran and of Khorshed Mansion for forty-six years and died on 22 November 1969.

Jamsetjee Madon was the great grandfather of our present Calcutta Zoroastrian Community's Religious & Charity Fund (CZCRCF) trustee, Cyrus Madan.

The late 1800s and early 1900s saw a great reform in religion with Dadabhai Naoroji leading the way with a call to return to the *Gathas*. He wanted to remove all Hindu customs which we were following and return to the belief of Zoroastrianism being a monotheist religion with a belief in one God, Ahura Mazda. Jamsetjee Madon was also a reformist. He was a trustee of Late D.B. Mehta's Zoroastrian Anjuman Atash Adaran and he supported the Head Priest, Dastur Kaikobad Aderbad Dastur Noshirwan, when he went to Rangoon from Calcutta to perform Bella's (the daughter of a Parsi mother and Goan father) navjote. When he died he bequeathed Bella Rs 5,000 to assist her in her court case (Obituary: Jamsetjee Framjee Madon [1923] *Parsi Prakash* vi, 113).

EARLY PARSIS OF CALCUTTA
(1880 ONWARDS)

Parsis came as refugees to India, became farmers, then became leaders in the opium trade with China, and later established cotton and jute mills. Striking wherever opportunity arose, in the 1880s they became famous for their trade in bangles, as suppliers to the railways, and as educationists and industrialists. The fact is that any business was acceptable and the list ranged from hosiery goods, paper, railway contracts, aerated water, tea packaging and wine shops to brokering on the stock exchange, selling roots, laundry and soap making. Even as professionals they excelled be it as geologists or painting, horse racing or the study of Avestan texts. One way or another the tradition of business, perseverance in the face of odds, and the willingness to try new ways of making money continued. More importantly, the need to educate children started gaining more prominence as Parsis realised the head start this gave in life.

Meherwanji Nanabhai Mehta was born in Navsari on Dhantaras day on 1 October 1857 in the home of his mother's father.

From 1868 to 1873 his father Nanabhai Manaji Mehta had the sub-contract of blasting rocks at Kasaraghat. The head contractor who had been entrusted with the job by GIP Railway, absconded with Rs 50,000 of the railways' money. Nanabhai had to leave Bombay and return to Navsari with his family.

Around this time Meherwanji's rich uncle Edalji Naoroji Mehta, who had a thriving business in China, came to Navsari. Meherwanji became his uncle's favourite and he was sent by his uncle to Calcutta

Meherwanji Nanabhai Mehta

Ratanbai Meherwanji Mehta

Pirojshah MN Mehta

to get a commercial training. Meherwanji studied at St. Xavier's College for three years.

In 1879 he joined a trading company but he was not happy. He wrote to his uncle Edalji requesting him to call him to China so he could start his own business. In reply, his uncle sent him thirteen cases of gold-plated glass bangles worth Rs 4,000. These Chinese gold bangles were very popular in India and thus started Meherwanji's glass bangle business. Soon he was known as the Bangle King of India.

Meherwanji developed a large import business with China, Japan, Germany and Australia.

In 1897 he went to China and opened a branch of his business there leaving his brother Dorabjee (grandfather of present CZCRCF trustee, Numazar D Mehta) in charge of his affairs in Calcutta.

Meherwanji was trapped in Germany during World War I in 1914 but managed to make his way back. In 1915 he went to Japan, opened a branch there and put his nephew Manaji in charge.

He started a glass factory in Calcutta named MN Mehta Glass Works and a match factory in Ootacamund. The machinery for which he paid Rs 60,000 was bought from Germany. Six Japanese experts were called from Japan to supervise the manufacturing.

He also had a business in hosiery goods and electronic goods. People said he had the Midas touch and anything he touched turned to gold.

In memory of his brother, Dorabjee Nanabhai Mehta, he built a maternity hospital in Navsari and created a fund for its maintenance. The DN Mehta Parsi Maternity Hospital was inaugurated on 17 January 1915 by the Sheriff of Bombay, the honourable Sir Jamshedji Jeejeebhoy, 5th Baronet.

Meherwanji contributed towards the building of the Atash Behram in Navsari and a building attached to it. He gave a large donation towards the purchase of the building called Navaz Bagh in Zap Street, Maleswar, Navsari. He made a new building for Mehta

Club in Navsari and he also gave his own house to the Rustomji Jamshedji Jeejeebhoy school. He donated generously to the Banaras Hindu University as well.

The Maharaj Sahab Gaekwad of Baroda awarded him the gold medal of 'datar mandal' on the occasion of his birthday darbar in 1916.

When he died at the age of seventy-one on 14 July 1928 he left behind six buildings in Calcutta, five in Kobe and Canton and a large palatial home in Navsari.

A large meeting of the entire Parsi Anjumans of Navsari was held in Khurshedwadi to mourn his death and to record the community's appreciation and gratitude, under the chairmanship of the head Desaiji Saheb Ardeshir Maneckji. A decision was taken to include his name in the list of those remembered in Zoroastrian prayers, to place his oil portrait in the main hall of the Navsari Atash Behram, and to install his statue at the Maternity Hospital. On 25 January 1930 Sir Phiroze Cursetji Sethna unveiled the statue and the portrait.

After Seth Meherwanji's death, his son Pirojshah Mehta looked after the family business. Unfortunately he did not make a success of it and in 1935 all his businesses had to be wound up.

Naoroji Jamaspji Arjani was born in Navsari in 1862. On the recommendation of his uncle, Framji Arjani, he came to Calcutta around 1883 and joined the company of Burjorji Fram Modi, first as an assistant and then as a manager. He worked here till he died in 1927.

He was a trustee of the Calcutta Zoroastrian Community's Religious & Charity Fund from 1901-1906 and from 1910-1927.

At the time of building the Late Ervad D.B. Mehta's Zoroastrian Anjuman Atash Adaran, he went to Bombay to collect funds for the construction of the building. He was one of the first trustees of the Adaran.

In 1912 when the new Tower of Silence was under construction, he would go every day to Beliaghata and supervise the work. He also supervised the Maneckji Rustomji Dharamsala and took an interest in the construction of Khorshed Madan Mansion. At the time of a death in the community, he would be the first person to help. Further he started the practice of printing the Parsi Directory of Calcutta.

Hormusji Burjorji Tangree had a thriving trade business with China. Hormusji imported glass bangles, Chinese preserves and coloured paper and traded under the company name of HB Tangree & Company.

Kaikhusroo H. Tangree was the eldest son of Hormusji. He was educated in Calcutta and he started a business in electric goods in 1921 called Hoshang Tangree & Company. They acquired contracts from the government and the railways and the company grew very rapidly. He built an office-cum-residence at Tangree House on Ezra Street. He died in 1967.

Dinshaw Sorabjee & Company

Two Parsis trading in Punjab, Dinshaw B Banaji and Sorabjee S Colah, obtained a railway contract in Bagula (now Bangladesh) from Bengal State Railway in 1885. They started the business in the name of Dinshaw Sorabjee & Company. They bagged contracts for serving the refreshment rooms in thirty-two stations in Bengal run by Bengal Dooars Railway and Darjeeling Himalayan Railway companies. They also obtained contracts for North Western Railway. Their original head office was at Saraghat. In 1915 when the bridge at Saraghat to Parbattipur was constructed, they shifted to Parbattipur. Finally, they shifted to Sealdah in 1935.

Sorabjee S Colah

At Saraghat, they had an aerated water factory and a tea packaging department. In 1897 they started dealing in wines and provisions.

Dinshaw Sorabjee & Company would serve free meals to all Parsi customers on the railways. When the Indian Railways took charge of their own catering business, this company came to an end but the wine shop still continues on Lower Circular Road.

Jamshedji Rustomji Saklat's father and grandfather had a thriving business in sacking and woollen cloth in Bombay. In between 1830-1860 they had sixteen large shops and several warehouses in Bazargate, Bombay. Their annual turnover was in crores. By 1875 this family had lost all its wealth and young Jamshedji came to Calcutta to work with Cawasji Edulji Khambatta. In 1882 he joined Singer Sewing Machine. In 1886 he joined Jamshedji Madan in a partnership known as Madan & Saklat Company. He was a leading member of the stock exchange.

He donated generously during his lifetime. He wanted girls to have the same educational opportunities that boys had and stipulated that his educational funds were for both boys and girls (women's education was just beginning around this time).

The Ravangah was constructed by Jamshedji's wife Nawajbai Saklat and his adopted son, Jehangirji Jeevanji Modi, in memory

Jamshedji Rustomji Saklat

Jehangirji Jeevanji Modi

of Jamshedji. It cost Rs 81,000 and it was entrusted to the Calcutta Zoroastrian Community's Religious & Charity Fund. They also built three buildings to house middle-income Parsi families.

Rustomji Kavasji Modi was born in 1868 in a poor family in Navsari. In 1907 he came to Calcutta to work at the branch of Hormusji Nusserwanji Cooper of Hong Kong. He wanted his wife to join him in Calcutta, but this was not allowed by the company, so he left his job. He started his own company 'RK Modi' out of his savings of Rs 500 and gradually amassed a great fortune.

Rustomji Kavasji Modi

He cornered the trade in a root called '*kooth*' which was grown in Kashmir and exported it to China. Rustomji also started a jute-baling press.

He built a palatial bungalow in Calcutta and when the Maharaja of Kashmir would visit, he would be Rustomji's house guest.

When the Atash Behram in Navsari was being built, he bore the expense of the building and the adjoining *dar-e-meher*. He opened a dispensary in Navsari in the name of his mother Pirojbai, built a large well and contributed generously to many public charities. He was a trustee of the Calcutta Zoroastrian Community's Religious & Charity Fund (1927-1936). He had two sons: Jal and Sorab.

Hormusji Ardeshir Kandawala was born in 1874 in a very rich family in Bombay. His father suffered huge losses in business and young Hormusji came to Calcutta to set up a laundry business in 1906. With financial assistance from a friend of the family, he set up his laundry at 1, Lindsay Street. The only other laundry in the city at that time was Major, Hill & Rogers, a European laundry at 25, Lindsay Street. Hormusji's business prospered and the European laundry just across the street had to close down. They sold out to Hormusji and left India. The Governor and the Viceroy were his patrons and he had customers from outside Calcutta as well.

He was keen to expand his business and, to obtain knowledge and experience, he visited UK and some other countries. As there was not enough place in his shop to launder large items like carpets, curtains, rugs, etc., the Gazdars, Edulji and Motabhai, gave him space in their workshop in Ghoosery.

This laundry was the only laundry which 'glazed' white caps. Later he started a factory to manufacture soap.

He was fond of sports and was a member of the 'Baronet Club'. He won prizes in athletics and cycling and also played cricket, billiard and chess. He started the Calcutta Parsi Club on the Maidan. He had a billiards table in his house where he practised daily and then participated in tournaments. The Calcutta Parsi Club first started functioning in his house.

He had knowledge of medicinal use of herbs and treated people free of charge. His three medicines for asthma were very effective. Many poor and sick people used to form lines daily near New Market and he would distribute his medicine there. He prepared medicine for leprosy which the suffering lepers queued up for daily. He was a bone setter too and provided all his services free of cost.

He was fond of reading and wrote many articles for Parsi journals under the pseudonym 'Hokayantra'.

Ervad Gustasp came to Calcutta in 1894 and joined Ralli Brothers in their cotton department. His son came with him. ***Tehmuras (Gustasp Tehmuras Dastur Meherjirana Tehmuras Gustasp)*** was only two years old when they arrived in 1894. He became a bank broker. His younger brother, Phiroze, became a company secretary and worked with the *Statesman Limited*.

Darashaw Nosherwan Wadia (25 October 1883 to 15 June 1969) was a pioneering geologist and among the first Indian scientists to work in the Geological Survey of India. He is remembered for his work on the stratigraphy of the Himalayas. He helped establish geological studies and investigation in India, at the Institute of Himalayan Geology which was renamed in 1976 after him as the Wadia Institute of Himalayan Geology. His seminal work *Geology of India* (1919) continues to be used by students.

He was born in Surat, then the family shifted to Baroda in 1894. His study was helped by the geological collection of the Maharaja

A commemorative Indian postal stamp released in 1984 with the portrait of DN Wadia

DN Wadia (1883-1969)

Sayajirao Gaekwad. At the age of twenty-three, he obtained the post of Professor of Geology at the Prince of Wales College, Jammu. In 1920 he joined the Geological Survey of India in Calcutta. He lectured at the Presidency College, Calcutta. He was Paleontologist at the Geographical Survey of India till 1938.

Darashaw received numerous awards for his work: the Back Award from the Royal Geographical Society in 1934, the Lyell Medal from the Geological Society of London in 1943, the Jayakishan Medal from the Indian Association for the Advancement of Science and other awards including the Padma Bhushan in 1958.

In 1951, a two-anna Indian postage stamp with a portrait of DN Wadia was released to commemorate 100 years of the Geological Survey of India.

He was the founder of the Parsi Zoroastrian Association and the Saklat Physical Culture Institute.

Erach A Bhiwandiwala was the eighth son of his poor parents. He had a great love of art and even before he could read and write, he could paint and draw. He began his life as an assistant in JF Madan & Company, on a meagre salary of Rs 10. He spent his spare time painting and he was given the privilege of admission to the studio of the great Bengali Master, JP Ganguli. He was a portrait artist. He went to England on a scholarship and studied under world-renowned masters: Sir John Lavery RA, Mr Henry Massey, Mons. Alfred Praga, RBA, Signor Dumini and others. He studied at the Chelsea Studio, the London

Erach A Bhiwandiwala, FRSA (Born 1898)

University College (Slade School) and at the Academie de la Cluse in Paris. In London, he got a scholarship from Northbrook Society and distinguished himself as Fellow of the Royal Society of Arts. He had the honour of being commissioned to make portraits of famous personalities such as the Countess of Howe (Curzon), Rt Hon. Mr George Lansbury, Sir FS Jackson MP, Sir Mancherjee Bhawnaggree MP, Lady Chelmsford, Mr Shaporjee Saklatwala, MP Sir Jamshedji Jeejeebhoy Bart, the Prince & Princess Kaya of Japan and others.

In the opinion of experts, Mr Bhiwandiwala had rediscovered the colour and the oil processors of the old masters and is one of the eminent sons of India who have shown the rest of the world the pre-eminence of Indian Art.

AC Ardeshir was the eldest son of Cooverji Ardeshir, the well-known mail contractor of the Deccan. He graduated in 1906 standing first and winning all prizes and scholarships in history. He was a fellow of the Deccan College from 1906-1908 while pursuing his masters. He took seriously to horse racing in 1927 and had the unique distinction of being the first Parsi to win the Classic Double at Calcutta, the King Emperor's Cup and the Viceroy's Cup with his famous Australian horse, Ethics. He won almost all the classic races for Arabs and thoroughbreds at Bombay and Poona, including the much-coveted Governor's Cup, the Byculla Club Cup, the Rajpipla Gold Cup, the CN Wadia Gold Cup and the Obidullah Khan Gold Cup.

He was a connoisseur of Indian art and had the finest private collection of Indian paintings in the world. He was an authority on Indian art as well.

Jehangir Cawasji Godiwala was born into a poor family in Bombay. He started life as a stenographer. Later he became a successful salesman for a company dealing in dental supplies.

AC Ardeshir leading in his famous Australian horse 'Ethics' who won the double classics at Calcutta – the King Emperor's Cup and the Viceroy's Cup in 1934. He is the first Parsi in the history of racing to win this double event

JC Godiwala
(Born 1901)

He started his own business in Calcutta in the name of JC Godiwala & Sons dealing in dental and medical supplies. Business was good and between 1931 and 1933, he bought over two well-known English and American firms in Calcutta dealing in the same goods. It was later known as the Associated Dental and Medical Supply Company, at 9, Chowringhee Road, Calcutta. The firm supplied material to India, Burma and Ceylon with agents operating in Madras, Rangoon and other important cities.

Dr Irach JS Taraporewala was born in 1884 in Hyderabad (Deccan). He studied law at the University of Cambridge and was barrister-at-law in London. A chance meeting with Professor Christian Bartholomae, Professor of Philology with a particular interest in Indo-Aryan languages, including Avesta and ancient Iranian studies, changed the course of his life. He left a lucrative career in law and moved from England to Germany to work under Professor Bartholomae for his PhD in Avestan texts, which he obtained in 1913.

Dr Irach JS Taraporewala

He returned to India before World War I to accept a chaired professorship of Comparative Philology in the linguistics department at the University of Calcutta. His tenure at the University of Calcutta ended when he moved to the Deccan College in 1940.

Dr Taraporewala translated the *Gathas* and his book *The Divine Songs of Zarathustra* was published in 1951. He speaks of Ahura Mazda as the one God and spreading Zoroastrianism to the seven continents. He would be extremely gratified to know of the resurgence of interest in the true message of Zarathustra and the *Gathas* that now exist. In his book, *The Divine Songs of Zarathustra,* he writes:

> The place of Zarathustra among the prophets is unique. He was born not merely to teach and uplift the Iranian race so many thousands of years ago, but his message was meant for all humanity and for all ages. For Zarathustra was not only the prophet of Iran but, He was the world teacher and this message is the eternal teaching of Truth, Love and Service. His message has a very special value for humanity today.

SETH EDULJI OLPADVALA AS NARRATED BY BURJOR MODI

Seth Edulji Olpadvala donated his house to the Calcutta Zoroastrian Community's Religious and Charity Fund. This bungalow at 52, Chowringhee Road was broken down and replaced by a multistorey building with a hall on the ground floor. The income from this building is the only source of funds for the Calcutta Zoroastrian Community's Religious and Charity Fund, which it uses for the upkeep and benefit of the Zoroastrian community in Calcutta.

Seth Edulji was born in Calcutta. When he was 18 years old, his father died and he had to take charge of the family business and did so very well.

He was a founder member of the Masonic Lodge Darius and he rose to become Master of the Lodge. He was a financial benefactor of the Calcutta Parsi Club and a trustee of the Calcutta Zoroastrian Community's Religious & Charity Fund.

Seth Edulji Olpadvala

But his favourite was the 'Pipla Club'. This was where the elite of the Parsis gathered each evening. They got together at the western end of the Queen's Way opposite the Victoria Memorial and sat under a large pipal tree on chairs which Edulji brought in the boot of his limousine.

Seth Edulji Olpadvala and his wife Ratanbai

Among the Parsi Sethias who gathered there were Sir Coyaji, Sir Ardesher Dalal, the Nalladaroos, the Mehtas, the Tangris, the Modis, the Nanavatis, the Drivers and Meherbai Madan. It was the ladies group of the Pipla Club who kept constantly urging Seth Edulji Olpadvala, Trustee of the Anjuman, to build a hall for the community as they found the halls of our two agiaries too small for holding weddings, navjotes and other functions and the Firpos, the Grand and the Great Eastern Hotel too expensive.

Then came the war. With it came cans of Coca Cola. Everybody feared the war but nobody realised the danger the tins of army Coca Cola were to bring to India's soft drinks industry. In time customs changed, dress changed, society changed, people changed. The Pipla Club was dwindling, whilst the Calcutta Parsi Club which opened its doors to ladies, grew from strength to strength. Defence took over a large part of the Maidan and the Pipla Club had to shift to the eastern end of Queen's Way. Red Road became a runway for the Spitfire and Hurricane Fighter Aircraft looking after the air defence of Calcutta. The Parsi Club was just outside the defence area. Baffle walls, air raid shelters were built, trenches dug, one just in front of our tennis lawns where the Judo Club now stands. Anti-aircraft guns nicknamed 'Ack Acks' were placed on high buildings, one on the museum just opposite the club. There was blackout enforced every night and off and on, the air raid signals blew. Nothing much happened till one day the Japanese bomber planes flew in from the east over Calcutta. It was an afternoon, we were at the Club, we ran and jumped into the trenches. There was terrible commotion and gunfire, but young Khurshed Tangree comforted us by saying, 'Don't worry, its only our ack ack guns firing'. From that day, heaven knows for what reason, he was fondly nicknamed 'Ack Ack Tangree'.

Those planes did drop a few bombs on Calcutta, but luckily missed the armament-carrying ship that was in Calcutta Port. Remember the Bombay explosion? Calcutta was lucky enough to just miss the same. But one bomb dropped on the timber yard next to Madan Mansion and scared the life out of the tenants. The next day they and many more Parsis joined in the great exodus out of Calcutta which in a week, was emptied of seventy per cent of its population, mostly hiking along the Grand Trunk Road out of Bengal.

The war ended but the 'Pipla Club' ladies who had by now also become members of the Calcutta Parsee Club, carried on their battle with the trustees to build a hall for the Parsis. Finally, they won. In 1967 Seth Edulji lost his wife Ratanbai, who had been an invalid, in bed for many years. Seth Edulji was lonely, he had no children. In a moment of philanthropic generosity, he gifted his magnificent mansion at 52, Chowringhee to the Anjuman Trustees with the request to build a hall for the Parsis after his death. But also insisting that as he was now living on Anjuman property, he would pay a rent of Rs 250 a month, which was a princely sum in those days. Very soon severe competition crippled both Byron Companies. All of Edulji's other assets were sold off to pay for his firm's debt. Unfortunately, the community did not know how badly Edulji's fortune had been wiped out as he had never complained. It was only a few weeks before his death that we learnt that he never had any money for his daily bazaar and he would give his cook a few knick-knacks from his collection to sell at throw-away prices to buy his daily needs. By then it was too late to help him and in 1971 he died a pauper.

This is a sad story of a good generous and rich man having to die in penury. The Lord has his ways and surely he will grant Seth Edulji's soul eternal peace. This then is the legacy he left behind. A legacy that has enriched us spiritually and morally, besides giving us our much-coveted Hall which is the pride of our community.

PADAMJI PESTONJI GINWALA

This noted Parsi barrister was an economist and a public figure in Bombay, later in Rangoon and then in Calcutta. He was Bella's lawyer in the Saklat Vs Bella case.

Padamji Pestonji Ginwala (1875-1962) was born in Ankleshwar and pursued his early education in Ahmedabad. He studied law at the University of Cambridge and was called to the Bar at Lincolns Inn in 1897. Then he moved back to India and started practice as an advocate in the Bombay High Court. He also served as a Professor of History and Economics at Elphinestone College from 1899-1900. In 1900, he shifted to Rangoon where he practised in the Chief Court of Lower Burma. He was Bella's lawyer in the Saklat Vs Bella case Suit No. 91 of 1915 of the Chief Court of Lower Burma. 'Parsi lawyers were involved in Bella's case at crucial points. Despite the tiny size of the Parsi community of Burma, two of her lawyers in Rangoon were Parsis – namely P.P. Ginwala and P.D. Patel.' (Mitra Sharafi, *Colonial Parsis and Law: A Cultural History. Government Research Fellowship Lectures 2009-2010)*

In 1916 he served as Secretary to the Burma Legislative Council and was also a member of the Indian Legislative Assembly from 1921-1923. He was the President of the Rangoon Municipal Corporation from 1921-1922. Later he served on the Indian Tariff Board from 1923-1930 for which he was knighted on 1 January 1927.

He was a delegate to the Imperial Conference in 1930. He was one of the members of the second Round Table Conference of

Pesi Ginwala

Hilla Ginwala

India in 1931, Ottawa Conference of 1932 and World Monetary and Economic Conference in 1933. He was an expert in fiscal and tariff affairs and headed many committees. He published an essay on Railway Electrification and Industrialisation, which was later published by the Indian Chamber of Commerce in 1945.

In 1945 he settled in Calcutta. He served as a Director of Indian Iron & Steel Company. He also served as President of Indian Institute of Metals. In 1963, a gold medal was established by Indian Institute of Metals in his memory, the *Sir Padamji Ginwala Gold Medal*, to recognise a candidate securing the highest marks in the Associate Memberships Examination (Part I) of the Institute.

His son Peston (Pesi) Padamji Ginwala (1919-2008) was also a senior barrister practising at the Calcutta High Court. He was a trustee of the RD Mehta Trust in Calcutta.

DHUNJEEBHOY BYRAMJEE MEHTA AND HIS DESCENDANTS

Dhunjeebhoy Byramjee Mehta was from a priestly family in Navsari which was ruled by the Gaekwad of Baroda upto Independence. The rule of law in Navsari was of the Gaekwads and not British Law.

He also followed the pattern of many wealthy Parsis by making his fortune in the opium trade with China, then investing in cotton and jute mills and playing a prominent role in society and politics. He had a close family and business connection with Jamshedji Tata.

His son Rustomji D Mehta bought the land for the dokhma in Calcutta and led the family in building the Late Ervad D.B. Mehta's Zoroastrian Anjuman Atash Adaran. The priest of his choice in the 'Tana' ceremony for the dokhma was Dastur Kaikhasru Jamaspjee, and for the consecration of the Atash Adaran was Dastur Kaikobad Aderbad Dastur Noshirwan. Both priests were reformists in their views.

Dhunjeebhoy Byramjee Mehta was born in Bombay. He came to Calcutta in 1846 to take charge of Behramji Cama & Company, as its manager. The company closed down following the failure of the Backbay scheme in Bombay. Dhunjeebhoy then started his own business, trading with China. One of Dhunjeebhoy's brothers, Kaikhusru Byramjee, was based out of Hong Kong. This business thrived and he made a fortune for himself. In 1860 he relocated his entire family to Calcutta.

On the advice of Jamshedji Tata, he started in 1877, the Empress of India Cotton Mills in Serampore, near Calcutta which employed many Parsis and Bengalis. Dhunjeebhoy and his son Rustomji went

Dhunjeebhoy Byramjee Mehta

Bai Khorshedbai Dhunjeebhoy Mehta

to Manchester, England to buy cotton-spinning machinery. After Dhunjeebhoy's death, this mill was destroyed in a fire. On his visits to England, Dhunjeebhoy and Rustomji came in close contact with Dadabhai Naoroji. Naoroji presided over a commercial firm in the UK that dealt in cotton and supplied machinery to some of the first Indians to set up cotton mills in the country.

Lord Canning, the Viceroy of India, had his residence at 55, Canning Street in Calcutta. When a new Government House (the present Raj Bhavan) was built, the Viceroy's office and household shifted there. Dhunjeebhoy promptly bought the house at 55, Canning Street.

In this house a separate place of worship (*dadgah*) was created in 1890. Three priests brought the '*alaat*' on foot from Navsari. The house in Canning Street was completely remodelled. This is now known as Mehta's Building. In 1912 this holy fire was shifted to the Late D.B. Mehta's Zoroastrian Anjuman Atash Adaran and the fire temple was consecrated by Dastur Kaikobad Aderbad Dastur Noshirwan.

In 1864 Dhunjeebhoy was appointed first trustee of the Calcutta Zoroastrian Community's Religious & Charity Fund.

Rustomji Dhunjeebhoy Byramjee Mehta

Rustomji Dhunjeebhoy Byramjee Mehta, son of DB Mehta, was awarded Companion of the Most Eminent Order of the British Empire by the British government. He was the Sheriff of Calcutta, a Trustee of the Port Trust, a first-class magistrate and Vice Council for Parsi Club. He was Chairman of Howrah Municipality and was a member of the Indian National Congress. He had six children: Maneck, Khurshed, Nusserwanji, Dossabhai, Jehangir and Najamai.

Rustomji began his career in an Armenian company, Messrs Apcar & Company. He then switched to his father's firm when he went to Hong Kong and Japan. In his house, in order to carry out Dhunjeebhoy's wishes, Bhagaria Mobeds from Navsari began a three-month odyssey transporting *alaat* (ritual objects and implements) overland to the eastern metropolis. When they reached the Hooghly river, then spanned only by a pontoon, predecessor of the Howrah Bridge, the priests took care to cross the waterway only at midnight and while wearing special sandals made of iron. By the turn of the century, the Empress of India Cotton Mills was a great commercial success and they diversified into jute. We find some mention of this in the *New York Times* (1902). 'The two great modern industries of India are cotton and jute.' 'The Petits and the Wadias had captured the cotton on the Bombay side. It remained for the Mehtas to cross over to the Bengal side and capture the jute.'

According to *The Cyclopedia of India*, a biographical dictionary from the early twentieth century, RD Mehta was recognised as a tower of strength by the Parsi community of Calcutta, who recognised in him their leader and the exponent of their views. This is relevant as this was the time of reform in religion. Scholars had realised that Zoroastrianism is a monotheist religion, with belief in

24 May 1891
R.D. Mehta to Dadabhai Naoroji
Naples, Italy
M-100 (5)
Two handwritten pages
Original: fair

[Seal:] R D M A CLEAR CONSCIENCE IS A SURE DEFENCE
55, CANNING STREET,
CALCUTTA.

B.I.S.N. Co's.
S.S. "India"
Naples May 24th/91

Dear Seth Dadabhai

I am on my way to England with my 2 sons whom I wish to bring up for the Civil Service; our friend Mr. Manmohan Ghose has written to his son to make all arrangements & I hope to receive a letter from him at Plymouth. We will D.V. [?] reach London, Albert Docks, on the 2nd or 3rd June & if you would kindly enroll me as an Hony. Member of either Northbrook or the National Liberal Club I would feel greatly obliged. My stay in England will not extend more than 3 or 4 months & during that time I shall be travelling at [sic] difference places,—Scotland & Lancashire. Where could I meet you in London? A reply in the care of the Agents Messrs. Weekes Phillips & Co., Plymouth will reach me properly

Trusting this will find you in perfect health.

Yours very sincly,
R.D. Mehta

Dadabhai Naoroji Esq.
National Liberal Club
London.

only one God. In the Trust Deed of the Mehta Agiari, RD Mehta specified which priest we were to follow: Dastur Kaikobad Aderbad Dastur Noshirwan, High Priest of the Deccan, a religious scholar and a reformist who went to Rangoon from Calcutta to perform Bella's (daughter of a Parsi mother and non-Parsi father) navjote.

RD Mehta was at the vanguard in all matters. He was involved in the Nationalist movement. He joined the Indian National Congress in 1866. He was a close friend of Dadabhai Naoroji who, when in Calcutta, would stay at his residence.

24 September 1906
R.D. Mehta to Dadabhai Naoroji
Calcutta
M-100 (7)
Two handwritten pages
Original: fair

[DN:] replied
25/10/1906

[Seal:] R D M A CLEAR CONSCIENCE IS A SURE DEFENCE
55, CANNING STREET,
CALCUTTA.
24th Septr. 1906

My dear Seth Dadabhai

We are pleased to learn that you have accepted the Presidentship of this year's Congress. The Bengalees are fighting among themselves & any one & every one poses as a Leader. In the lot we have some very good men & some self seeking. I am sure your presence would tend to settle the matter down smoothly. We will take it as a great favor if you will put up with us as you so very kindly did on your last visit. Pray accept this as an invitation from my dear old parents & all of us. We would not say how very pleased we would be to put you up and to show you your likeness gracing and ornamenting our agiary.

By last mail I have sent my fifth son Khusroo for medical tuition with his eldest brother Maneck, the barrister whom I dare say you know. My barrister son Maneck aspires to a Judgeship of an High Court & I have to solicit your kind help in the matter. Need I say how grateful we all would be by our helping him & putting him in the way.

I sincerely trust you are keeping well & with our united kindest regards & best wishes,

I am,
Yours Sincerely,
R.D. Mehta

Stone Laying in Calcutta

In 1910 Rustomji donated land for the construction of a Dokhma in Calcutta, at Beliaghata. The Dokhma was consecrated by Dasturji Kaikhasru Jamaspjee (great great grandfather of our new Head Priest, Jamasp Jamaspasa), Head Priest of Calcutta Banaji Agiari. Earlier, in 1903, he had performed the navjote of Susuane Briere and her wedding to Ratan Tata by Parsi rites in the presence of sixty priests including high priests and Dastur Hoshang Jamasp, High Priest of the Deccan. ('A Parsi Convert', *Times of India*, 14 February 1903).

TOWER OF SILENCE.

Stone-Laying at Calcutta.

CALCUTTA, December 27.

The ceremony of laying the foundation of the new Tower of Silence at Beliaghatta on a piece of land recently secured through the exertions of Mr. R. D. Mehta, C.I.E., was performed by a Parsi High Priest, Dastoor Kaikhasroo Jamaspashana, assisted by his deputy Erwad Pirozshaw Mehrji Rana and other Priests of the Banaji Fire Temple of Calcutta. The ceremony was witnessed by about 800 Parsi ladies and gentlemen with their children. Before the ceremony came to a close a farewell contribution was made by everyone present and will ultimately be distributed equally amongst the various priests in charge of the two local Fire Temples. The High Priest brought the proceedings to a close with a sermon in which he dwelt upon the importance of the consecration of the Tower of Silence and exhorted his hearers to be staunch to their ancestral faith. In conclusion he thanked them for attending and specially those, numbering about 300, who had come to Calcutta from various parts of India at great personal inconvenience. The head trustee, Mr. C. M. Rustomjee, gave a history of the new tower and conveyed the thanks of the tower committee to all who had come forward with their voluntary contributions. He referred to the special services of Messrs. J. F. Madon, J. R. Saklath and K. Cowasjee, in their combined efforts to bring the tower project to a successful issue. Mr. J. F. Madon on behalf of himself and other members of the tower committee returned thanks.

The entire congregation then adjourned to a specially constructed pavilion where arrangements had been made to provide a banquet by the tower committee. After the usual loyal toasts and others the health of the High Priest was proposed and he was thanked for accepting the invitation to come from Bombay to lay the foundation stone. The High Priest having replied to the toast he and his deputy were then presented with shawls and cheques for considerable amounts by the Parsi residents of Calcutta. The High Priest will deliver a special lecture for Parsis at the Corinthian Theatre to-day, in the evening he leaves on a short visit for Darjeeling where he will be the guest of Mr. J. F. Madon.

TOWER OF SILENCE
Stone-Laying at Calcutta.

CALCUTTA. December 27 1910. The ceremony of laying the foundation of the new Tower of Silence at Beliaghata on a piece of land recently sourced through the exertions of Mr. R.D. Mehta, C.I.E., was performed by a Parsi High Priest, Dastoor Kaikhasroo Jamaspashana, assisted by his deputy Erwad Pirozshaw Mehrji Rana and other Priests of the Banaji Fire Temple of Calcutta. The ceremony was witnessed by about 800 Parsi ladies and gentlemen with their children. Before the ceremony came to a close, a farewell contribution was made by everyone present and will ultimately be distributed equally amongst the various priests in charge of the two local Fire Temples. The High Priest brought the proceedings to a close with a sermon in which he dwelt upon the importance of the consecration of the Tower of Silence and exhorted his hearers to be staunch to their ancestral faith. In conclusion he thanked them for attending and specially those, numbering about 300, who had come to Calcutta from various parts of India at great personal inconvenience. The head trustee, Mr. C.M. Rustomjee, gave a history of the new tower and conveyed the thanks of the tower committee to all who had come forward with their voluntary contributions. He referred to the special services of Messrs. J.F. Madon, J.R. Saklath and K. Cowasjee, in their combined efforts to bring the tower project to a successful issue. Mr. J.F. Madon on behalf of himself and other members of the tower committee returned thanks.

The entire congregation then adjourned to a specially constructed pavilion where arrangements had been made to provide a banquet by the tower committee. After the usual loyal toasts and others the health of the High Priest was proposed and he was thanked for accepting the invitation to come from Bombay to lay the foundation stone. The High Priest having replied to the toast he and his deputy were then presented with shawls and cheques for considerable amounts by the Parsi residents of Calcutta. The High Priest will deliver a special lecture for Parsis at the Coronthian Theatre today, in the evening he leaves on a short visit for Darjeeling where he will be the guest of Mr. J.F. Madon.

CURSETJI RUSTOMJI SETHNA AND DINBAI (NÉE MEHTA, DAUGHTER OF DB MEHTA) AND THEIR FAMILY

DB Mehta's daughter, Dinbai, married Cursetji Sethna. The Sethna family were closely connected with the Bhuggasarth sect of priests and all their children were trustees of the Anjuman Atash Behram of the priests of the Bhuggasarth sect. Ratan D Tata and Susuane Briere's wedding was performed in the Sethna house in the presence of sixty priests. The presence of sixty priests when only two are required must have been a strong statement of solidarity at that time.

Cursetji Rustomji Sethna was the husband of Dinbai Dhunjeebhoy Mehta, daughter of DB Mehta and Khorshedbai of the Calcutta Mehta Agiari. He had four sons: Sir Phiroze Cursetji Sethna (who married Banoo Sett), Dr Dossabhoy, Seth Hormusji, Shavakshaw; and two daughters: Homai and Khorshedbanu.

Cursetji Sethna died on 2 September 1890. There was a note in *Jam-e-Jamshed* on 28 August 1916 by Rustomji Pestonji Karaka in the section *Aaj konni baj chhe* in which the following was written about Cursetji:

Sir Phiroze Cursetji Sethna

> 1839-1891: Initially he acquired some training in business matters at William Simms & Company, and then went to Burma on behalf

of SP Dhanjibhoy & Company (DB Mehta's Company). After returning, he started his own trade, particularly with Burma in the name of C Rustomji Sethna.

He had opened his own branch in Rangoon. He also traded with Calicut, Calcutta and China. One of his son's (later Sir) Phiroze C Sethna attained fame in business and public life. He (Sir Phiroze Cursetji Sethna) became the President of Bombay Municipality Corporation in 1915-16 and presently is a member of the Legislative Council.

Sir Phiroze Cursetji Sethna, MBE Kt, BA, JP, OBE was the son of Dinbai (daughter of DB Mehta & Khorshed) and Cursetji Rustomji Sethna. He is one of the most famous Parsi sons of Calcutta. Phiroze, together with his mother Dinbai, grandmother Khorshed, uncle Rustomji Mehta and cousin Maneck Mehta, collected funds and donated them towards the building of the Late Ervad D.B. Mehta's Zoroastrian Anjuman Atash Adaran, the fire temple made in memory of his grandfather.

He married ***Banoo Sett***, daughter of Ardeshir Sett. She was educated up to the fourth standard and was an intelligent lady, both honest and straightforward. Mrs Banoo Phiroze Sethna was the Honorary Magistrate and Arbitration Officer in Bombay in the year 1949. She was also the Chief of the Bombay Honorary Presidency Magistrate Society in 1950 and a delegate at the Parsi Chief Matrimonial Court. Banoo's sister, Navaz, married Ratan J Tata. The Tata and Mehta families were very close. When Ratan D Tata married Susaune Briere, the navjote and wedding were conducted in the Sethna house at Hornby Road. The priest who performed the wedding, was the Calcutta Head Priest, Dastur Kaikhasru Jamaspjee, in the presence of sixty other priests of Navsari and Dastur Hoshang Jamaspji, High Priest of the Deccan.

The **Hon. Sir Phiroze Sethna** is a Member of the Council of State and one of the leading moderate politicians of India. Having been also appointed on the Joint Select Committee, he is now in London giving his share in moulding the political future of India. And well may he do so, for, it was his ancestor Rustam Manek who had introduced the British to the great court of Aurangzeb for gaining important privileges which led to the founding of their great empire in India. He is a life member of the Iran League, and is taking a keen interest in Persia.

جناب اجل سر فیروز ستنا عضو شو راي دولتي و یکی از سیاسیین اعتدالی عمدهٔ هندوستان است و چون چندیست بعضویت کمیته منتخبه هم معین گردیده اکنون در لندن متوقف و در تشکیل سیاست آینده هند سهیم و شریك میباشد چون جدش رستم مانك بود که دولت بریتانیا را از برای تحصیل امتیاز مهمي که منجر بتأسیس سلطنت بزرگ این دولت در هند گردیده بدربار عظیم اورنگ زیب معرفی نمود امید کامل انکه او هم از عهدهٔ کار خود بر آمده استعداد ذاتی و موروثي خود را ابراز نماید

The Iran League Quarterly
Journal of the Iranian Association

Sir Phiroze Cursetji Sethna had incredible achievements in different walks of life: commerce, politics, social and community leadership. Phiroze was the eldest son of Cursetji and Dinbai. His other siblings were Dr Dossabhoy, Shavakshaw, Hormusji, Homai and Khorshed.

He was born on 8 October 1867 in Bombay and accompanied his grandparents Dhunjeebhoy and Khorshed Mehta to Calcutta when he was six years old in 1873. He did his schooling from St Xavier's School, Calcutta and graduated from St Xavier's College in 1887 with a bachelor's degree in arts.

His father's poor health ensured that after graduation, he had to join the family business of purchasing cotton from up-country mills. After his father's death, he started a cotton mill, but suffered heavy losses. Thus he looked for opportunities elsewhere. He worked with Sun Life Assurance Company of Canada, which he served for thirty-three years. Recognised as an expert in the insurance business, he was appointed by the government as a member of the Insurance Experts Committee in 1936. He would walk down Churchgate Street daily in long coat and *pheta* (which all Parsis wore in those days) and accost every man he met with the query: 'Are you insured?' So persistent was he and so punctual in his daily appearance on the street that, far from being a joke and later a nuisance, it became a regular feature of his routine and people gradually began to look forward to seeing him. He became known as the insurance man of Churchgate Street and, in course of time, developed connections which grew sufficiently to place him at the very top of the business of insurance in this country as head of one of the greatest insurance concerns of the world.

Sun Life and Sir Phiroze

Sun Life of Canada was prominent among the foreign offices during this period because of a great personality connected with the company. He was Sir Phiroze Sethna, an institution by himself. He acted as Director of a large number of Boards of Companies and his was no perfunctory membership. He took deep interest and was noted for his meticulous attention to detail and accuracy in his business activities. His presence on a Board was almost a guarantee for the public and many business ventures flourished because of their association with this Parsi gentleman. Sir Phiroze epitomised one of the most remarkable examples of success attained by grit and perseverance. After graduation in 1887, he joined his father's business and worked as a *mukadam* in their cotton firm. Young Phiroze did not relish this work and his experience made him a little despondent. An interesting incident took place when he consulted a colleague who suggested to him that it was hopeless for a beardless youth to expect success in competition with older stalwarts of the cotton ring. Phiroze promptly retired into seclusion to grow a beard and moustache which he kept for the rest of his life. With these new acquisitions, he emerged once more into the fray but with no better success than before. After a few years of vain effort in this line he decided to enter the field of insurance and resolved to succeed.

Phiroze was a director of the Central Bank of India and later chairman and managing director for seventeen years, from 1921 till his death in 1938. He was connected with the Swedish Match Trust and took keen interest in the aviation and cinema industry. He founded Bombay Talkies and was President of the Motion Picture Association from 1936-1938. He was a director in Tata Iron & Steel, New India Assurance, Bombay Telephones, Bombay Steam Navigation, Union Bank of India, Andhra Valley Power, Indian Cement, Indian National Airways, Western India Match Company and various cotton and industrial units. For a man who lived in Calcutta, he had several posts in western Bombay-related firms.

His role in industrial development can be judged by the fact that the then Congress President, Subhas Chandra Bose, termed his death as a 'serious blow to industrial life'.

About politics he said: 'In politics I have throughout been a liberal.' He was close to Gopal Krishna Gokhale and Phirozeshah Mehta. He along with some others formed the 'National Liberal Foundation' in 1920, one of the three leading parties in India.

He served on the Bombay Municipal Corporation for many years and in 1915-1916, was the President of the Corporation. He was a Justice of Peace and also the Sheriff of Bombay. In 1921 he was elected by the British as a representative to the first Council of State in the Central Legislature.

Sir Phiroze Cursetji Sethna consistently demanded Indianisation of the defence department and reduction of defence expenditure. He was a member of the Sandhurst Committee and a member of the Indian Goodwill Delegation to South Africa. He was an arbritation officer for nearly twenty years and was made an Honorary Magistrate.

He was a leading Freemason and was Grand Master Depute of all Scottish Freemasonry in India. He was also Senior Grand Deacon of the Grand Lodge of Scotland. He was a member of the Rotary too.

He proposed a bill in 1934 for 'Parsi Marriage & Divorce' which was passed in 1936. He was a delegate to the Parsi Matrimonial Court and a trustee of the Mumbai Parsi Panchayat from 1931 till his death. He was a trustee of the Anjuman Atash Behram, Sir Ratan Tata Charities, Nusserwanji M Petit Charities and other trusts. He was the administrative head of the Bhuggasarth sect and arranged the function for the felicitation of Dr Hoshang Jamaspji (High Priest of the Deccan). In matters of religion, he wanted to bring Zoroastrianism back to its pristine purity and was an honoured life member of the Journal of the Iranian Association. He firmly believed Zoroastrianism was a monotheistic religion.

Sir Phiroze and Banoo had a daughter named Tehmina who married Faroukh Erach Bharucha who was the grandson of Ervad Sheriarji Dadabhoy Bharucha, an eminent Zoroastrian scholar who in the Petit Vs Jeejeebhoy case, gave evidence to support the petitioners 'that a person born in another religion and duly converted to Zoroastrianism and admitted into the religion, is entitled to the benefits of the religious institutions and funds mentioned in the plaint'. They had three daughters: Pilloo, Silloo and Aloo.

Pilloo married Paramasiva Prabhakar Kumaramangalam (Padma Vibhushan), who was 6th Chief of the Army Staff of the Indian Army (1966-1969).

In 1906 Phiroze had a serious railway accident in England and Her Majesty the Queen regularly made very gracious enquiries about his health. He was awarded an OBE in 1916 and a knighthood in 1926.

Mr Edwin Howard, speaking at his condolence meeting said: 'Mr Sethna speaks with swift fluency and so loudly that his attacks on the government are flung back by the echoing walls like machine gun salvos.' As a businessman, he naturally delighted in taking the government to task on financial and army expenditure.

Dr Dossabhoy Cursetji Sethna was the second son of Dinbai and Cursetji, born in 1868. He passed his SSC in fine Arts in Calcutta and then went to the University of Edinburgh in 1892 to study medicine. He was the first Parsi to get the degree of MB CM (Bachelor of Medicine, Master of Surgery) in 1896. In 1897 he passed ML (Licentiate in Medicine) from the Rotunda Hospital, Dublin, Ireland. He acquired special training in gynaecology and was the first Indian to work there as a house surgeon. He returned to Bombay in 1898.

Dr Dossabhoy died in 1932 and a building was donated in his name at Tardeo, Bombay in the compound of the Zoroastrian Building Society.

Shavakshaw Cursetji Sethna was born on 15 December 1869. He was the manager of Empress of India Cotton Mills at Bajbaj (now Budge Budge) near Calcutta. He served Bajbaj Municipality as a leading civilian. The Municipality named a road – 'Sethna Road' – in his honour.

Hormusji Cursetji Sethna was the fourth son of Cursetji and Dinbai. He worked with his elder brother. On 14 February 1929 two burglars entered their house and he was attacked with a knife. The story as reported in the *Sanj Vartaman* stated:

> Yesterday, there was an attack on a noble citizen and prominent businessman, Seth Hormusji. He is working in the cotton business along with his elder brother, the politician, the Hon'ble Sir Phiroze Cursetjee Sethna. Last night, at around 2.15 a.m, two burglars entered his house and attacked him brutally with knives causing four wounds. From among these, a wound in his left lung was quite deep and we are very sorry to report that he is in a very critical condition.
>
> Seth Hormusji stays at the rear side on the second floor of Canada building, Hornby Road with his mother Dinbai Cursetjee Sethna. Sir Phiroze's offices are also located in the same building. Lately their sister Mrs Homai Maneckji Rustomji Mehta (Calcuttawala) has arrived and was sleeping with her mother in her room. There are two gates to the building. Both were closed. It seems that the burglar or burglars entered last night through the windows by climbing the water pipes.
>
> When the robbers entered, Mr Hormusji got up. On seeing the intruder standing there he must have started fighting with him. The police believe that during their combat they came to the passage near the room of his mother. Mr Hormusji himself is not in a position to speak and verify anything.
>
> Meanwhile his sister heard his voice and came out. She saw that Hormusji was bleeding profusely and that the passage was full of blood. She tried to hold him and keep him from falling. She called

the servants and they rushed to help and made him lie down. Mrs. Mehta immediately phoned her brother, Dr Dosabhoy Sethna. She also called Dr Dadi Guzder who felt the need of a surgeon and called upon Dr Cooper. Along with him Dr Rustom Billimoria, Dr Phiroze Bharucha, Dr NH Vakil, Dr Modi and Dr Jurush Bharucha have started his treatment and are trying hard to save him.

The wound in Mr Hormusji's left lung is quite serious and he is in a very critical condition, which has resulted in great sadness. He is about 45 years of age. He has a very kind and gentle personality and has a huge circle of friends. On hearing the news, since morning numerous relatives and friends from other communities such as Hindus, Muslims, Englishmen and businessmen, etc., have been visiting the hospital and enquiring of his well being. This is truly an alarming instance of the robbery, theft and break-ins that are occurring in Bombay.

After injuring Mr Hormusji in a grievous manner, the burglar while climbing down the pipe accidently fell down into the street and died immediately. The police took the dead body in their possession. The victim looked like a Manglorean Hindu. We are not able to know if there was anybody else along with him as Seth Hormusji is unconscious.

Hormusji built a pavilion of the Doongerwadi (Tower of Silence) in memory of his father Cursetji Rustomji Sethna and also provided the furniture. He also gave two houses at Slater Road as a gift to the community after the death of his mother Dinbai.

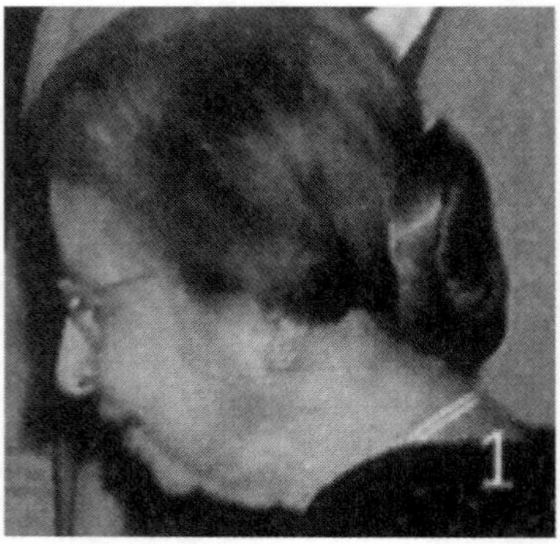

Homai Cursetji Sethna

He was a trustee of the Bhuggasarth Amelioration Fund,

member of the Anjuman Atash Behram Committee; he built a recreation hall at Dharampore in memory of his brother Phiroze Cursetji Sethna.

Homai Cursetji Sethna married her cousin Maneck Rustomji Mehta, son of Rustomji Dhunjeebhoy Mehta (brother of Dinbai). She was closely associated with many institutions in Calcutta and in appreciation of her services, she was awarded a Silver Medal by the Governor when the Prince and Princess of Wales came to India (1905-1906). She served as a volunteer during the Great War of Europe (1914-1919) and was presented another Silver Medal for her services. In 1919 she was conferred the title of MBE (Member of the Order of the British Empire). In 1926 the government awarded her the Silver Kaiser-i-Hind Medal in recognition of her public service.

Jalbhoy Ardeshir Sett had two daughters: Banoo, who married Phiroze Cursetji Sethna, and Navaz, who married Ratan J Tata. He did not have a son so he adopted his younger brother Jal as his son as a *Palak*.

In 1898 the Anjuman Atash Adaran was consecrated for the Bhuggasarth priests in Bombay by funds collected by Jalbhoy Ardeshir Sett as a leader of the Bhuggasarth sect.

Jalbhoy Ardeshir Sett, Phiroze Cursetji Sethna and Homi Cursetji Sethna were all trustees of the Anjuman Atash Behram.

Khorshed Rustomji Maneckji Mehta was the daughter of Jamshedji Madan. She was married to Rustomji Maneckji Mehta (great grandson of DB Mehta). She and Rustomji had three children: Serah, Shirin and Soli. Serah married Naval Jhaveri and they had a son, Russi. Russi's two sons, Neville and Yan, are the only two surviving members of the family today. Khorshed died on 14 January 1920 at a very young age. Her father Jamshedji Madan

Khorshed Rustomji Maneckji Mehta

Rustomji Maneckji Mehta

built the Khorshed Madan Mansion in her memory and presented it to the Calcutta Zoroastrian Community's Religious & Charity Fund to provide housing to the poor middle-class families.

Soli married Tehmina Patel, sister of Jeroo Postwalla. They had no children.

THE BANAJI AND MEHTA AGIARIS OF CALCUTTA

*The **Banaji Agiari** was consecrated in 1839 and the **Mehta Agiari** in 1912. The Banaji and Mehta families were both well-to-do families in Calcutta. There seems to have been a keen personal dispute between the families and this was played out in the court rooms and is reported widely in the Press as the 'Consular Defamation Case'. This personal rivalry may have influenced DB Mehta to start another place of worship in Calcutta.*

The Banaji Agiari was run by a private trust and unfortunately now there is no family member to look after it. The Agiari premises have been encroached upon and is now an electric market.

Foundation stone of the Banaji Agiari

Plaque at the Banaji Agiari

The Late Ervad D.B. Mehta's Zoroastrian Anjuman Atash Adaran was constructed with funds (Rs 67,000) collected by his wife Khorshedbai, by his daughter Dinbai (wife of C. Sethna), his grandson Phiroze Cursetji Sethna, by his son Rustomji D Mehta and by grandson Maneckji R Mehta, and from funds collected by the public (Rs 60,490).

When the Late Ervad D.B. Mehta's Zoroastrian Anjuman Atash Adaran Trust Deed was incorporated, the reform movement in our religion had just started and there was a sharp divide between the reformists and the orthodox members. The Late Ervad D.B. Mehta's Zoroastrian Anjuman Atash Adaran Trust Deed states:

> Dastur Kaikobad Aderbad Dastur Noshirwan shall be the first Head Dastur of the said Atash Adaran, and Shamsul-Ulama Sardar Dastur Kaikobad Aderbad Dastur Nosherwan, the present incumbent of the first named office shall be the first Head Senshai Dastur of the said Atash Adaran, and the said Head Senshai Dastur

The Banaji Agiari at present

> of the said Atash Adaran shall examine into, regulate and control the religious rites, ceremonies and services of the said Adaran.

Dastur Kaikobad Aderbad Dastur Noshirwan performed Bella's navjote in 1914 and he also addressed the Parliament of World Religions in 1924, where he spoke of the Universality of the Zoroastrian religion.

The Banaji Agiari declared Heritage Property by the Govt. of West Bengal

The Banaji Agiari well

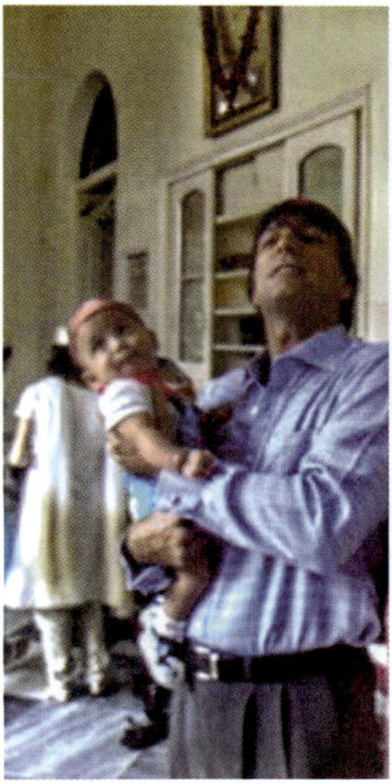

ABOVE: *Mr Noshir Tankariwala with Dastur Dr Firoze Kotwal at the entrance of the D.B. Mehta Agiari*

LEFT: *Noomi Mehta and baby Samara on the first floor of the Late Ervad D.B. Mehta's Zoroastrian Anjuman Atash Adaran*

Plaque at the D.B. Mehta Agiari

Entrance of the D.B. Mehta Agiari

Donations received from members of the community on the occasion of the centenary of the Late Ervad D.B. Mehta's Zoroastrian Anjuman Atash Adaran

THE DB MEHTA AND JAMSHEDJI TATA FAMILY CONNECTION

Ratan D Tata and Susaune Briere's wedding and navjote were performed at the Sethna house in Bombay. Sixty priests attended the wedding to show their support for the event. It must be remembered that the Gathas *had only been recently translated and the learned priests knew that Zoroastrianism was a monotheistic religion meant for all mankind.*

The Late Ervad D.B. Mehta's Zoroastrian Anjuman Atash Adaran is the only functioning Fire Temple in the city of Kolkata today. DB Mehta and Jamshedji Tata's families were very close businesswise and as families. Jamshedji Tata and Dhunjeebhoy Mehta quite likely met at Dadabhai Naoroji's house in England. Jamshedji Tata set up the Empress Mills in Nagpur; Phiroze Cursetji Sethna (grandson of DB Mehta) and his brother set up the Empress Mills in Budge Budge and Serampore.

DB Mehta

Dadabhai Naoroji

Jamshedji Tata

Phiroze C Sethna

Ratan J Tata

Navazbai Tata

Ratan D Tata
Photo courtesy: Parsiana Publications

Susaune Briere
Photo courtesy: Parsiana Publications

JRD Tata
(son of Ratan D Tata & Susaune Briere)

Phiroze Cursetji Sethna and Ratan J Tata were brothers-in-law having married the Sett sisters: Banoobai and Navazbai.

Ratan D Tata's wedding to Susaune Briere took place in the Sethna house at Hornby Road.

Letters of Sooni Tata written to her mother (courtesy of JRD Tata Papers, Tata Central Archives, Pune):

> *Dear Mama, I have a very important news to tell you. By the time you receive this letter, it will already have been 15 days that I will have been a Parsi—a real one wearing a Kosti. It was only yesterday that I knew. Ratan had always told me that it was impossible but that if at all it was possible, the decision might be made suddenly. Mr Sethna and Mr Kanga were in charge of the matter. I suddenly got word from Ratan's office that if I were to learn the necessary prayers, in 3 or 4 days it could all be over. I was completely taken by surprise but I immediately started to learn the prayers and I recited all evening long the prayers in Palavi. Luckily in Navsari, Ratan had already taught me two of the smaller ones. The official sanction had been given by the high priest only this morning. Ratan wants the ceremonies on Sunday. It will be attended by a whole lot of important Parsis and will take place at Mr. Sethna's. Like the little girl in Navsari, I will wear a [---] and be wrapped in a white cashmere shawl. But what is most significant is that at the same time the priest will marry us and nobody will give me another thought. I will be allowed to enter the temple (which I couldn't do before) or stay in a house where a Parsi lies dead. If a Parsi dies in a house, all non-Parsis even if they were tenants in the same house have to leave it until the body is carried away. I am a bit confused by all the stir that this is causing. Not in the last 300 or 400 years has such a case as this been disputed. Luckily the press is for us. A Dastoor is going to come and teach me the important prayers. I will recite them to you in Paris, Mama, and you will see how strange they sound. Ratan's mother is coming down from Navsari for*

the ceremony. I will be dressed all in white. For it is agreed that I will be already dressed in my new sudra and blouse. It is only the kusti that the dastoor will tie around my waist.

(1903 Bombay, Wed)

Darling mother – Here I am, at last a Parsi. Everybody is happy for me and so am I. I spent five sleepless nights filling my head with the prayers I had to learn – now I feel exhausted. Let me however try and recount the ceremonies of my conversion and our marriage that took place at Mr Sethna's big house. At 4 pm I was made to sit in a small room next to the huge salon in Mr Sethna's house where the ceremony was going to be performed. A dastur with his face hidden sat opposite me. I recited some prayers with him, ate a piece of pomegranate and then raised to my lips in a gesture of sipping a cup of pewter which contained the urine of the cow. It is supposed to purify but of course nobody really drinks it—not even touch it with their lips—but it is a custom that has existed since the beginning. Ratan asked me not to tell you about this (he finds it distasteful). Don't therefore talk of it. Normally, a dastoor is present but this time, he remained on the other side of the partition. The wife of a dastur and the beautiful Meherbai Tata were with me. They dressed me in an (ijar) and confined my hair in a (matte bonu) and draped a white cashmere shawl around my shoulders. Then feeling very pale and nervous, and with my feet in sapats I entered the drawing room where there were waiting at least 60 dasturs when only one is really necessary. I was made to sit with my back to everyone facing the high priest and I started to recite the prayers with him. After 15 minutes or so, he placed my hands in the sleeves of the sudra and left, then all the Parsi ladies, the wife of Mr Kanga, the daughters of Meherbai and the wife of the dastur held up before me a white sheet to shield me from view. I put on the sudra, my blouse and a white sari with a silver border. When I was ready, the High Priest returned but this time we stood—he

standing just behind me. Then, while I held his little fingers, he tied the kusti around me. Then seated again there were more prayers with the priest showering my head with pieces of pomegranate, coconut. There it ended and I was led into the midst of all our friends who were waiting to congratulate me. Soon only our close friends remained and the drawing room was prepared for our wedding which had to take place before sunset. I read out aloud, the pledge to the Zoro faitehr, in French, and then the ceremony began. Ratan and I sitting side by side and the dasturs started to pray and showering us with rice. It took about 25 minutes. When everybody except the family and Mr Kanga had left, we all drank champagne and then quietly we returned home.
(From the French original text, 1903)

DASTUR KAIKHASRU JAMASPJEE

Dastur Kaikhasru Jamaspjee was a highly educated reformist priest. He performed Susaune Briere's navjote and wedding to Ratan D Tata. In the Petit Vs Jeejeebhoy case, he was questioned in court:

'Would you now admit Mrs. Tata [Susaune Briere] into the fire temple of which you are the Head Priest?'

He replied: 'As she has become a Zoroastrian I would have no objection.' (From the Parsi Panchayat case, 7th February 1908, Beamen's Notebook. Suit No. 689-06.)

A view – very rarely seen – of the Zoroastrian Ritual consecrating the foundation of a new Tower of Silence in Calcutta, 1910. The 'Tana' ceremony is here depicted with intricate threading plan of the Foundation

This ceremony was performed on 25 December 1910. A rare performance, it will be memorable for the fact that both the sects of the Parsi priests participated therein shoulder to shoulder. The Kadimi Priests of Surat and Shahanshai Priests of Navsari acted under the guidance of a Bombay High Priest. This is the first of such co-operation recorded. The picture gives a view of the intricate ritual requiring great skill in laying out a ground plan inter-twined by threads round a mass of nails – a sort of magnetic charmed field over which the later structure is built for the disposal of the dead among the Parsis

A unique group photograph of the Priests present at Calcutta at the time of Consecration of the Foundation of the New Tower of Silence (1910)

The late Dastur Kaikhasru Jamaspjee is in the centre. Next to him is Minochere Jamaspjee. Next to him on the left is Erwad Erachsha Bomanji Kumana who was the Chief Director of the ceremonies. Close behind him is standing Erwad Merwanji K. Beheram Kamdin Dasturna (Author of Athornan Nama*). On the left of Dastur Kaikhasru is Ervad Burjorji J. Dastur Meherji Rana, the priest-in-charge of the Mehta Anjuman Fire Temple of Calcutta*

The photograph depicts a unique event as it represents both the sects of the Parsi Priests uniting in a common Consecration ritual – a rare sight much to be admired

Navsari was the stronghold of the Zoroastrian religion in India. ***Dastur Kaikhasru Jamaspjee***, our Calcutta High Priest of the Banaji Agiari, was from the Bhuggasarth sect of priests of Navsari and he was also High Priest of the Anjuman Atash Behram, Bombay, High Priest of the Banaji Atash Behram, High Priest of Cama Agiari, Soda Bottlewala Agiari and Godiwala Agiari, High Priest of Colombo, Lahore, Aden and Lunouli. He performed the Tana ceremony of the Tower of Silence on land purchased by RD Mehta.

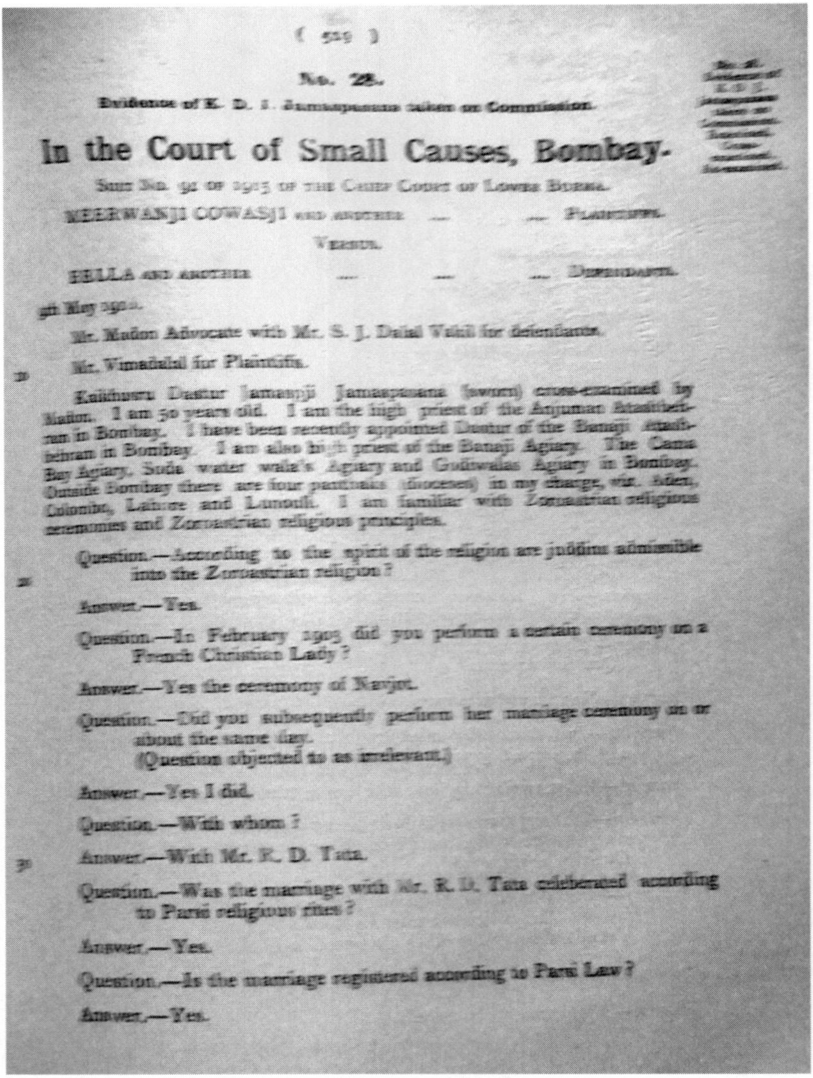

No. 28.

Evidence of K. D. J. Jamaspasana taken on Commission.

In the Court of Small Causes, Bombay.

Suit No. 91 of 1915 of the Chief Court of Lower Burma.

MEERWANJI COWASJI and another ... ... Plaintiffs.

Versus.

BELLA and another ... ... Defendants.

9th May 1910.

Mr. Mahon Advocate with Mr. S. J. Dalal Vakil for defendants.

Mr. Vimadalal for Plaintiffs.

Kaikhusru Dastur Jamaspji Jamaspasana (sworn) cross-examined by Mahon. I am 50 years old. I am the high priest of the Anjuman Atash-behram in Bombay. I have been recently appointed Dastur of the Banaji Atash-behram in Bombay. I am also high priest of the Banaji Agiary. The Cama Bag Agiary, Soda water wala's Agiary and Godiwalas Agiary in Bombay. Outside Bombay there are four panthaks (dioceses) in my charge, viz. Aden, Colombo, Lahore and Lonouli. I am familiar with Zoroastrian religious ceremonies and Zoroastrian religious principles.

Question.—According to the spirit of the religion are juddins admissible into the Zoroastrian religion?

Answer.—Yes.

Question.—In February 1903 did you perform a certain ceremony on a French Christian Lady?

Answer.—Yes the ceremony of Navjot.

Question.—Did you subsequently perform her marriage ceremony on or about the same day.
(Question objected to as irrelevant.)

Answer.—Yes I did.

Question.—With whom?

Answer.—With Mr. R. D. Tata.

Question.—Was the marriage with Mr. R. D. Tata celebrated according to Parsi religious rites?

Answer.—Yes.

Question.—Is the marriage registered according to Parsi Law?

Answer.—Yes.

Cross examination of Dastur Kaikhasru Jamaspjee in Saklat Vs Bella

EXHIBIT 66.

True extract from the Registrar of Parsi Marriages, filed before Commissioner.

Exhibit 66. True extract from the Registrar of Parsee Marriages filed before Commissioner. 11-5-1916.

EXHIBIT 66.

SUIT No. 91 OF 1915 CHIEF COURT LOWER BURMA.

R. S. DADACHANJI.

Commissioner.

15th May 1916.

Extract from the Register under Section 601 Act XV of 1865, of Parsi Marriages solemnized within the Local limits of the Ordinary Civil Jurisdiction of His Majesty's High Court of Judicature at Bombay.

Date and place of Marriage.		Names of the Husband and wife.	Condition at the time of Marriage.	Rank or Profession.	Age.	Residence.	Names of Fathers or Guardians.	Rank or Profession.	Signature of the officiating Priests.	Signatures of the witnesses.	Signatures of Father or Guardian when Husband and wife is an infant.
8th Feby. 1903.	Bombay Altamont Cumballa Hill.	Ruttonjee Dadabhoy Tata.	Widower.	Merchant.	46	Fort Hornby Row	Father of the husband Dadadhoy Cowasjee Tata.	Dead.	Kaikhasru Dastur Jamaspjee.	In native characters.	R.D. Tata.
		Susaune now named Soonabai Briere.	Spinster.		23		Father of the wife Paul Briere.	Merchant.	Minochere Dastur Jamaspjee.	In native characters.	Soonabai R.D. Tata.

I do hereby certify that the above is a correct entry of the original Certificate deposited with me.

True Extract,

N. D. GARDA,

Registrar of Parsee Marriages.

Bombay, 11th May 1916.

(Sd.) B. DADABHOY,

Registrar of Parsee Marriages under Act XV of 1865.

Bombay 1st April 1903.

(295)

Wedding certificate of Susuane Briere and Ratan Dadabhoy Tata

Dastur Kaikhasru Jamaspjee and Dastur Minochere Jamaspjee performed the navjote and then the wedding ceremony of Susaune Briere and Ratan Tata.

The Late Ervad D.B. Mehta's Zoroastrian Anjuman Atash Adaran Trust Deed says it is 'for the celebration of religious and other rites & ceremonies therein, in the manner and according to the tenet of the Parsi Zoroastrian Bhuggasarth Mobeds of the principle Atash Behram of Navsari in the territory of his Highness, the Gaekwad of Baroda'.

This is relevant for in 1915 Baroda was an independent territory under the Gaekwad of Baroda. 'The situation was different in the princely state of the Gaekwad of Baroda, where the laws of 1865 found no application and the Panchayats, still partially dominated by priests, practiced their traditional function up till India's independence.' (Eckehard Kulke, *The Parsis in India*)

The Dokhma was built by Hormusjee Nusserwanji Cooper, a merchant partly based in Hong Kong. The laying of the Dokhma's foundation was a big event in the community and about 800 Parsis attended. After the ceremony, Dastur Kaikhasru Jamaspjee, Calcutta High Priest, gave a talk at Dharamtalla Street's Corinthian Theatre, owned by Jamsetjee Framjee Madon.

DASTUR KAIKOBAD ADERBAD DASTUR NOSHIRWAN

Dastur Kaikobad Aderbad Dastur Noshirwan was the Head Priest of the Late Ervad D.B. Mehta's Zoroastrian Anjuman Atash Adaran. The Trust Deed states that the Parsis of Calcutta have to follow him while observing their religious rites.

Here's an excerpt of the cross examination of Dastur Kaikobad Aderbad Dastur Noshirwan during the trial of Saklat Vs Bella:

Q. Then why did you take Bella to be a Parsi child?
A. Because her mother was a Parsi.

Asked if the fire temple would be descecrated if Bella entered the fire temple before her navjote, he replied: 'No.'

Q. Why not?
A. Because she is born of a Parsi parent.
Q. You mean a Parsi mother?
A. Yes.

Dastur Kaikobad Aderbad Dastur Noshirwan was the first Head Priest of the Late Ervad D.B. Mehta's Zoroastrian Anjuman Atash Adaran and it was consecrated by him in 1912. He was the High Priest of the Deccan which was under the rule of the Gaekwad of Baroda. He was a priest of the Bhuggasarth sect of Navsari. He presided over the first Zoroastrian Conference organised by Dastur Dhalla in 1910. He was made Sham-il-ulema at the Delhi Coronation

Durbar on the visit of the new Monarch, George V – a prestigious recognition. He was a Pahlavi scholar and wrote and translated many religious books including *Avesta Shabde No Mool* (The Origin of the Avesta). The famous scholar of the Pahlavi language Dr West termed it as 'requiring extreme attention'. An issue of the magazine *Raast Goftar,* dated 8 September 1901, carried the following citation:

'Dastur Kaikobad Noshirwan Jamasp Aashana has undertaken a very informative topic of exploring the root of Avesta and we are of the opinion that he has more or less reached the point of success, so also will be acknowledged by our Parsi as well as European scholars.'

In the year 1903, the Honourable Government granted him the respect of appointing him the Honorary Magistrate of Poona.

He became the High Priest of the Deccan on 25 April 1908 after the demise of Sardar Dastur Hoshang Jamasp. Within three months of his appointment in July 1908, the Honourable Government bestowed upon him the title of the First Grade Sardar of the Deccan; the excellent quality of Dasturji and his nobleness was highly appreciated in government circles and he was conferred the title of 'Private Honorary'. This was mentioned in the English and Gujarati papers.

> The Head Priest of the Deccan, Dastur Kaikobad Aderbad Dastur Noshirwanji has been appointed as the Sardar of the first grade by the Honourable Government. The rank of Head Priest should be considered more than any other governmental honours despite the fact that the Parsis of Poona and Deccan will not be able to conceal their joy upon the achievement of their Head Priest. Dastur Kaikobad is truly worthy of this honour. (*Tawarikhe-Dastoor Jamasp Ashana*)

An extract from *Jam-e-Jamshed* dated 21 July 1908:

FIGURE 6:
"A TORRENT OF FIRE"
[*Hindi Punch* (6 September 1914), 16.]
[By permission of the British Library (SV 576).]

A Torrent of Fire [Hindi Punch (6 September 1914), 16.]

> Two Dastur Sahebs—Dastur Nosherwanji Jamaspji and his brother Dastur Hoshangji— held the position of the first grade of the Dasturs. Presently their successor, the new Dastur Kaikobad Aderbad Dastur Nosherwan has also been conferred with the honour of being decorated as the Sardar of the First Grade by the Honourable Government and has spread joy and cheer in the community. We have been observing that this Dastur family of Poona has won laurels and honour because of their wisdom, ability and determination. The native place of that family is Navsari and as a rule, the Athornan tribe of Navsari has been a success wherever they have been because of the wisdom of their heart. However, the Jamaspasa family of Poona have gained their fame due to their knowledge of the religion of their progressive habits in keeping with the current trends and considering it as their ardent duty to make their tribesmen achieve progress. Dasturs could be found in plenty today, but those that guide their tribe in accordance with the advanced knowledge of their religion, to stride on the true path, are not known to be found except...those daring Dasturs from Poona.

He was the High Priest of the Deccan, Malwa, Calcutta and Madras and the twenty-three diocese (*panthaks*) under his charge. In 1914 Dastur Kaikobad went from Calcutta to Rangoon, to do the navjote of Bella (daughter of a Parsi mother and non-Parsi father).

Calcutta's Late Ervad D.B. Mehta's Zoroastrian Anjuman Atash Adaran Trust Deed states that Dastur Kaikobad Aderbad Dastur Noshirwan 'shall examine into and regulate and control the religious rites, ceremonies and services of the said Atash Adaran'.

EXHIBIT A 2.

Telegram, D. Kaikobad to Meherwanji (Cowasjee) filed before Commissioner.

EXHIBIT A 2.

Suit No. 91 of 1915 Chief Court, Lower Burma

Exhibit A 2. Telegram. D. Kaikobad to Meherwanj (Cowasjee) filed before Commissioner. 10-3-1914.

R. S. DADACHANJI,
Commissioner.
12th May 1916.

INDIAN TELEGRAPHS.

To

HON'BLE MERWANJI,

Rangoon.

With due deference to your worthy self I must stick to my promise have performed similar Navjots after resolution of panchayet I am an Independent dastur Kaikobad.

21)

Telegram sent by Dastur Kaikobad Aderbad Dastur Noshirwan, Saklat Vs Bella

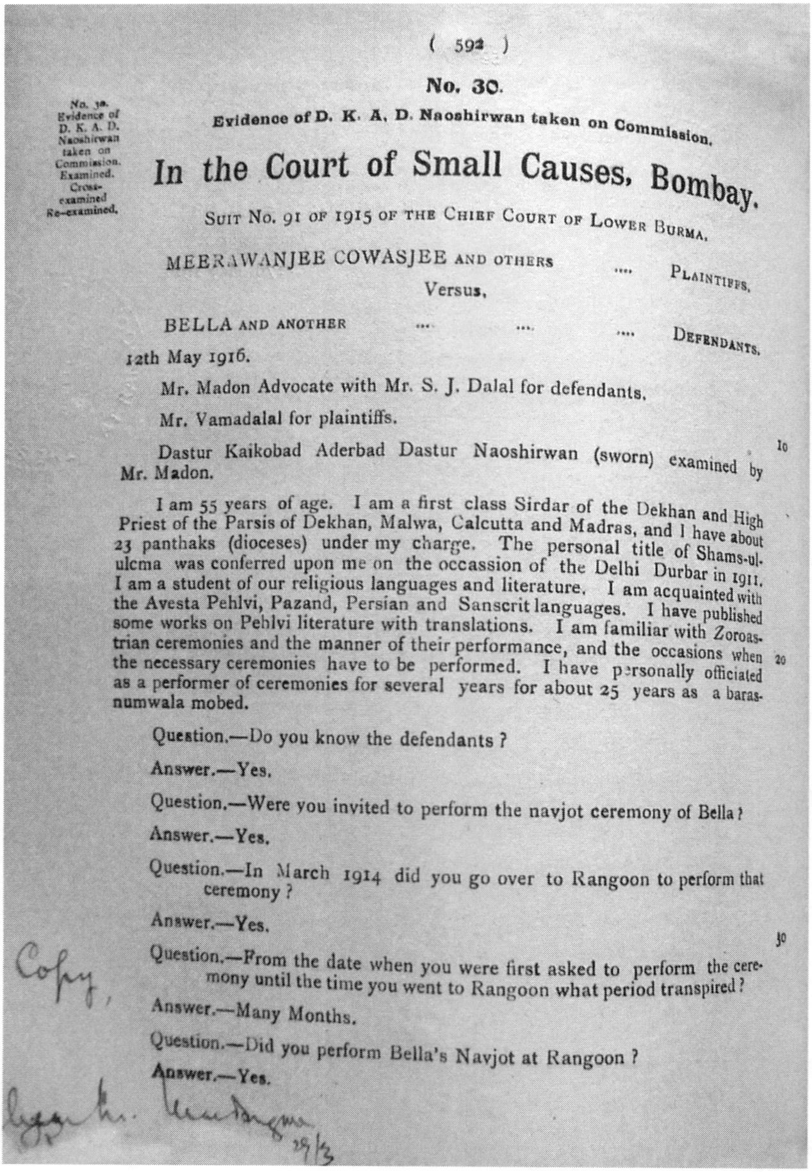

(592)

No. 30.

No. 30. Evidence of D. K. A. D. Naoshirwan taken on Commission. Examined. Cross-examined Re-examined.

Evidence of D. K. A. D. Naoshirwan taken on Commission.

In the Court of Small Causes, Bombay.

SUIT No. 91 OF 1915 OF THE CHIEF COURT OF LOWER BURMA.

MEERAWANJEE COWASJEE AND OTHERS .... PLAINTIFFS.

Versus.

BELLA AND ANOTHER .... DEFENDANTS.

12th May 1916.

Mr. Madon Advocate with Mr. S. J. Dalal for defendants.

Mr. Vamadalal for plaintiffs.

Dastur Kaikobad Aderbad Dastur Naoshirwan (sworn) examined by Mr. Madon.

I am 55 years of age. I am a first class Sirdar of the Dekhan and High Priest of the Parsis of Dekhan, Malwa, Calcutta and Madras, and I have about 23 panthaks (dioceses) under my charge. The personal title of Shams-ul-ulema was conferred upon me on the occassion of the Delhi Durbar in 1911. I am a student of our religious languages and literature. I am acquainted with the Avesta Pehlvi, Pazand, Persian and Sanscrit languages. I have published some works on Pehlvi literature with translations. I am familiar with Zoroastrian ceremonies and the manner of their performance, and the occasions when the necessary ceremonies have to be performed. I have personally officiated as a performer of ceremonies for several years for about 25 years as a barasnumwala mobed.

Question.—Do you know the defendants ?

Answer.—Yes.

Question.—Were you invited to perform the navjot ceremony of Bella ?

Answer.—Yes.

Question.—In March 1914 did you go over to Rangoon to perform that ceremony ?

Answer.—Yes.

Question.—From the date when you were first asked to perform the ceremony until the time you went to Rangoon what period transpired ?

Answer.—Many Months.

Question.—Did you perform Bella's Navjot at Rangoon ?

Answer.—Yes.

Copy,

Cross examination of Dastur Kaikobad Aderbad Dastur Noshirwan in Saklat Vs Bella

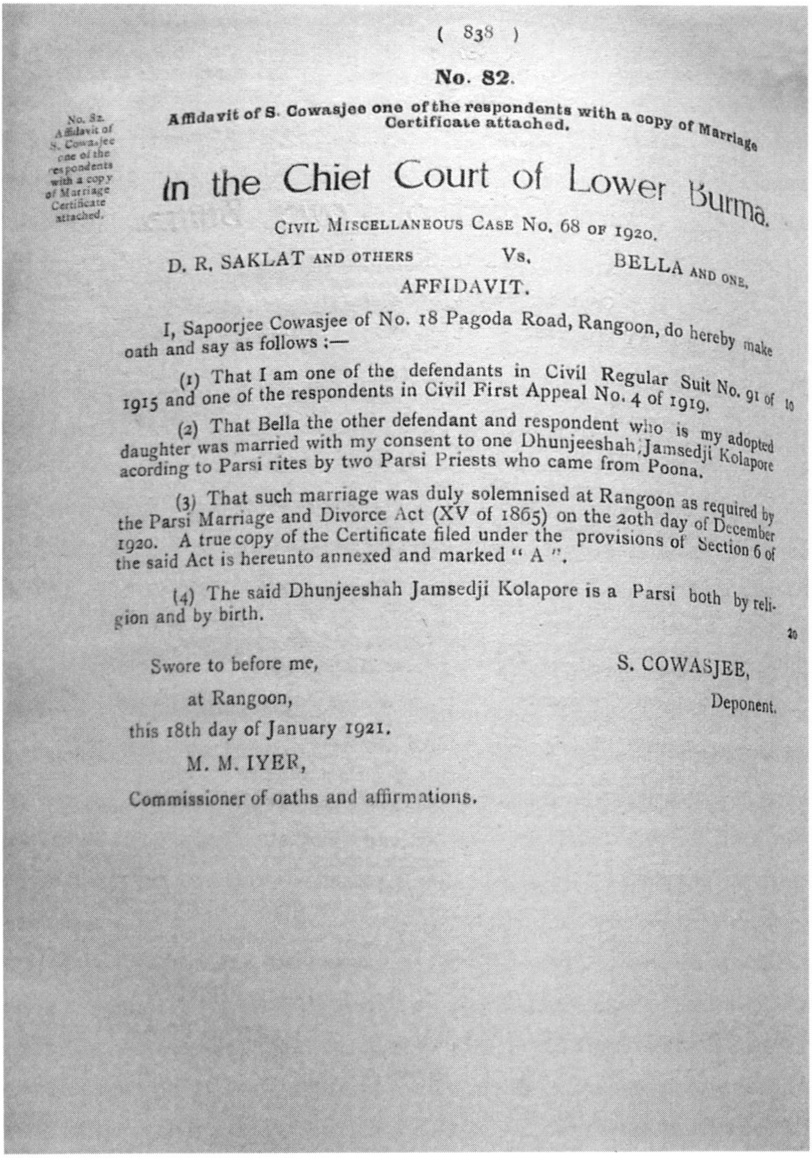

(838)

No. 82.

No. 82. Affidavit of S. Cowasjee one of the respondents with a copy of Marriage Certificate attached.

Affidavit of S. Cowasjee one of the respondents with a copy of Marriage Certificate attached.

In the Chief Court of Lower Burma.

CIVIL MISCELLANEOUS CASE No. 68 OF 1920.

D. R. SAKLAT AND OTHERS Vs. BELLA AND ONE.

AFFIDAVIT.

I, Sapoorjee Cowasjee of No. 18 Pagoda Road, Rangoon, do hereby make oath and say as follows :—

(1) That I am one of the defendants in Civil Regular Suit No. 91 of 1915 and one of the respondents in Civil First Appeal No. 4 of 1919.

(2) That Bella the other defendant and respondent who is my adopted daughter was married with my consent to one Dhunjeeshah Jamsedji Kolapore acording to Parsi rites by two Parsi Priests who came from Poona.

(3) That such marriage was duly solemnised at Rangoon as required by the Parsi Marriage and Divorce Act (XV of 1865) on the 20th day of December 1920. A true copy of the Certificate filed under the provisions of Section 6 of the said Act is hereunto annexed and marked " A ".

(4) The said Dhunjeeshah Jamsedji Kolapore is a Parsi both by religion and by birth.

Swore to before me, S. COWASJEE,

at Rangoon, Deponent.

this 18th day of January 1921.

M. M. IYER,

Commissioner of oaths and affirmations.

Affidavit of Bella's uncle Sapoorjee Cowasjee in Saklat Vs Bella

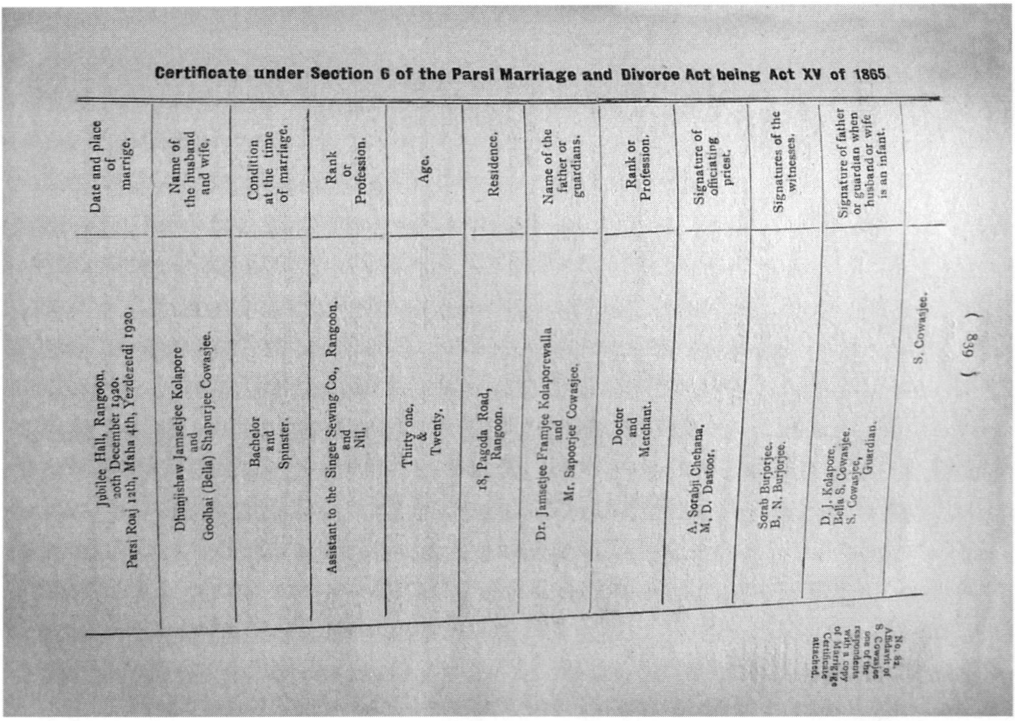

Certificate under Section 6 of the Parsi Marriage and Divorce Act being Act XV of 1865

Date and place of marrige.	Jubilee Hall, Rangoon, 20th December 1920. Parsi Roaj 12th, Maha 4th, Yezdezerdi 1920.
Name of the husband and wife.	Dhunjishaw Jamsetjee Kolapore and Goolbai (Bella) Shapurjee Cowasjee.
Condition at the time of marriage.	Bachelor and Spinster.
Rank or Profession.	Assistant to the Singer Sewing Co., Rangoon. and Nil.
Age.	Thirty one, & Twenty.
Residence.	18, Pagoda Road, Rangoon.
Name of the father or guardians.	Dr. Jamsetjee Framjee Kolaporewalla and Mr. Sapoorjee Cowasjee.
Rank or Profession.	Doctor and Merchant.
Signature of officiating priest.	A. Sorabji Chehana, M. D. Dastoor.
Signatures of the witnesses.	Sorab Burjorjee. B. N. Burjorjee.
Signature of father or guardian when husband or wife is an infant.	D. J. Kolapore. Bella S. Cowasjee. S. Cowasjee, Guardian.
	S. Cowasjee.

No. 82, Affidavit of S Cowasjee one of the respondents with a copy of Marriage Certificate attached.

(839)

Bella married Dhunjishaw Kolapore in December 1920 by Parsi religious rites and the wedding was registered under the Parsi Marriage and Divorce Act. The wedding was performed by the Bhuggasarth priests from Poona. They accepted Bella as a Parsi

LAW AND PARSI IDENTITY

Saklat Vs Bella and Petit Vs Jeejeebhoy: Two legal cases fought in the early 1900s have helped define who is a Parsi. But one has to remember that as late as 1915 the 'obiter dictum' *defining the word Parsi given by Justice Davar was not accepted as law. The words 'Parsi' and 'Zoroastrian' were being used interchangeably.*

Interestingly, in both the cases, the priests who performed the navjote ceremony (of Bella and Susaune Briere) were the Head Priests of Calcutta, one of the (now defunct) Banaji Atash Adaran, and one, the first Head Priest of the Late Ervad D.B. Mehta's Zoroastrian Anjuman Atash Adaran. The petitioners in the Petit Vs Jeejeebhoy case who wanted Susaune Briere to be accepted as a Parsi were all connected with Calcutta.

In **Petit Vs Jeejeebhoy,** the petitioners asked for the right of a person born in another religion and converted to Zoroastrianism, to be entitled to the benefits of the religious institutions and funds. It is interesting to note the distinguished section of people who took up cudgels on behalf of this case. We are talking of the crème de la crème of Parsi society in those days.

The Petitioners were:

- RD Tata (who married Susaune Briere and whose navjote and wedding by Parsi rites were performed by the Head Priest of Calcutta, Dastur Kaikhasru Jamaspjee, in the Sethna house).

- Ratan J Tata (brother-in-law of DB Mehta's grandson, Phiroze Cursetji Sethna).
- RD Sethna (brother-in-law of Dinbai Sethna [née Mehta, daughter of DB Mehta of Mehta Atash Adaran] and trustee of the Anjuman Atash Behram of the Bhuggasarth sect).
- NN Katrak (trustee of the Anjuman Atash Behram run by the Bhuggasarth sect).
- Dinshaw Maneckji Petit (who donated the Petit Library to the Calcutta Zoroastrian Community's Religious & Charity Fund).
- Rustomji Byramji Jeejeebhoy (who donated generously to the Calcutta Zoroastrian Community's Religious & Charity Fund).

It is also worth noting that the petitioners were as anxious as anybody else to follow the rules of the Parsi tradition. Ratan D Tata had first converted Susaune to the Zoroastrian religion and then married her according to Parsi rites. He sought and followed the advice of Dastur Dorab Peshotanji Sanjana and Ervad Jivanji Jamshedji Modi, Secretary of the Bombay Parsi Panchayat, in letters addressed to him on 8 February 1903. He now wanted his wife to be accepted as a member of the community.

This case was never decided in court as the ladies who were complainants were not party to the suit.

What is of relevance to the Parsis of Calcutta is that the Plaintiffs were community members connected with Calcutta, and they wanted her to be accepted and that the priest who performed the ceremonies, was the High Priest of Calcutta, a Head Priest of the Bhuggasarth sect, who performed the ceremony in the presence of sixty other priests including the High Priest of the Deccan, Dastur Hoshang Jamasp. In simple terms the most honourable members of the then Parsi community and the most revered priests held these opinions, despite the brouhaha created by the media and the (perhaps unenlightened) adverse opinion of the common man.

In the **Saklat Vs Bella** case, two judgments were delivered in 1918 and 1920, in favour of Bella. Finally in 1924 the case went on appeal to the Privy Council. By this time, Bella's adopted father, Sapoorjee Cowasjee, had passed away and there was no one to fight her case. Even in 1924 when the final verdict was given, the judge declared: 'But, upon the whole, their lordships feel that the plaintiffs have failed in the greater part of their suit, and that giving to them of a declaration is an indulgence .... and that a declaration be made, namely that Bella was not entitled as of right, to use the temple' ... 'But if the trustees choose to permit her this of itself furnishes no ground of complaint.'

This case is relevant to Calcutta as it establishes the meaning of the term 'Parsi' in the city in 1915 when the Trust Deed of the Late Ervad D.B. Mehta's Zoroastrian Anjuman Atash Adaran was incorporated.

Dastur Kaikobad Aderbad Dastur Noshirwan, whom the trust deed enjoins the community in Calcutta to observe in our religious rites and practices, held the opinion that Bella was a Parsi as her mother was a Parsi. His statement was recorded in court.

Dastur Kaikobad Aderbad Dastur Noshirwan went from Calcutta, where he was attending his brother-in-law's wedding, to Rangoon to do Bella's navjote in 1914. At that time, Mr Jamsetjee Framjee Madon, one of the first trustees of the Late D.B. Mehta's Zoroastrian Anjuman Atash Adaran and one of the pioneers of Indian cinema, advised him to 'perform the navjote if one of the parents was a Parsi'.

It seems like in the early 1900s there was little doubt about what our attitude should be to people who wanted to join the community through bona fide marriage and the sincerity of purpose to pursue the religion. It is strange that, over a century later, we are still debating the problem and coming up with solutions that are more conservative than those pronounced before!

PARSI ZOROASTRIAN

Who is a Parsi Zoroastrian and what was the Bhuggasarth priests' understanding of this nomenclature? NN Katrak, trustee of the Anjuman Atash Behram, gave his views in court. Dastur Kaikobad Aderbad Dastur Noshirwan (High Priest of the Deccan and Calcutta) said: 'Bella is a Parsi, because her mother was Parsi.'

Dastur Kaikhasru Jamaspjee (High Priest of the Anjuman Atash Behram and of Calcutta) said he would allow Mrs Tata (Susaune Briere) to enter the agiari: 'As she has become a Zoroastrian, I would have no objection.'

We produce below actual pages of the transcript of the court case that took place at the time. We believe that reading the actual words and the affirmations made by those defending these actions might have more of an impact than just our verbal summaries from these transcripts.

In his cross examination in Saklat Vs Bella, NN Katrak, trustee of the Anjuman Atash Behram, of the priests of the Bhuggasarth sect explains the meaning of the term Parsi/Zoroastrian.

Dastur Kaikobad Aderbad Dastur Noshirwan, Head Priest of Calcutta, who did Bella's navjote and Dastur Kaikhasru Jamaspjee, Head Priest of Banaji Agiari, who did Susaune Briere's navjote were also Head Priests of the Bhuggasarth sect.

Nanabhoy Nowrojee Katrak, trustee of the Anjuman Atash Behram, and one of the Plaintiffs in Petit Vs Jeejeebhoy, in his cross examination answered in court:

(540)

No. 29.

No. 29. Evidence of N. N. Katrak taken on Commission. Examined, Cross-examined, Re-examined

Evidence of N. N. Katrak taken on Commission.

In the Court of Small Causes, Bombay.

SUIT NO. 91 OF 1915 OF THE CHIEF COURT OF LOWER BURMA.

MERWANJEE COWASJEE & OTHERS ... PLAINTIFFS.

Versus

BELLA & ANOTHER .... DEFENDANTS.

10th May 1916.

Mr. Madon, Advocate with Mr. S. J. Dalal for Defendants.

Mr. Vimadalal for plaintiffs.

NANABHOY NOWROJEE KATRAK, Sworn.

Examined by Mr. Madon.

I am 58 years old. I am an L. M. & S. of the Bombay University. A Justice of the Peace and Honorary Presidency Magistrate of Bombay. I am Vice-President of the Committee and a Trustee of the Anjuman Atash-Behram of Bombay. I am also a trustee of the People's Free Reading Room and Library and of other Charities in Bombay. I am a member of the Managing Committee of the Rahnumaye Sabha and also one of its trustees. I am one of the Secretaries and also one of the Trustees of the Zoroastrian Conference. I am a treasurer of the Iranian Association. Member of other Zoroastrian Societies. I was for 15 years a member of the Bombay Municipal Corporation and for about 10 years a member of its Standing Committee of which I was Chairman for one year.

Question.—Do you take an interest in Parsi questions religious and social ?

Answer.—Yes.

Question.—Do you move in Parsi Society and in Bombay Society generally ?

Answer.—Yes.

Question.—Are you acquainted with Parsi usages and with the general opinions of the Parsi community ?

Answer.—Yes.

Question.—Were you a member of the Juddin Committee appointed in 1903.

Answer.—I was a member of that Committee as also of its Sub-Committee.

Cross examination of NN Katrak, Trustee, Anjuman Atash Behram in Saklat Vs Bella

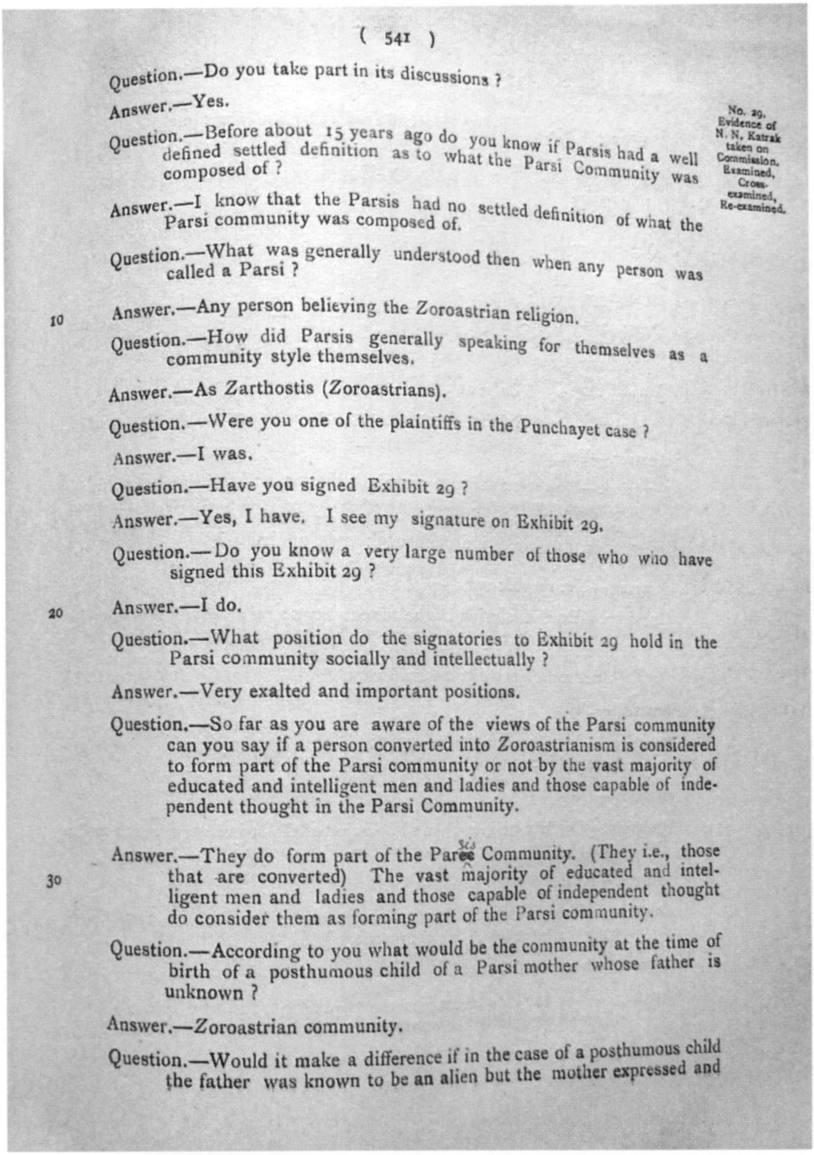

(541)

Question.—Do you take part in its discussions ?

Answer.—Yes.

Question.—Before about 15 years ago do you know if Parsis had a well defined settled definition as to what the Parsi Community was composed of ?

No. 29. Evidence of N. N. Katrak taken on Commission. Examined, Cross-examined, Re-examined.

Answer.—I know that the Parsis had no settled definition of what the Parsi community was composed of.

Question.—What was generally understood then when any person was called a Parsi ?

Answer.—Any person believing the Zoroastrian religion.

Question.—How did Parsis generally speaking for themselves as a community style themselves.

Answer.—As Zarthostis (Zoroastrians).

Question.—Were you one of the plaintiffs in the Punchayet case ?

Answer.—I was.

Question.—Have you signed Exhibit 29 ?

Answer.—Yes, I have. I see my signature on Exhibit 29.

Question.—Do you know a very large number of those who who have signed this Exhibit 29 ?

Answer.—I do.

Question.—What position do the signatories to Exhibit 29 hold in the Parsi community socially and intellectually ?

Answer.—Very exalted and important positions.

Question.—So far as you are aware of the views of the Parsi community can you say if a person converted into Zoroastrianism is considered to form part of the Parsi community or not by the vast majority of educated and intelligent men and ladies and those capable of independent thought in the Parsi Community.

Answer.—They do form part of the Parsis Community. (They i.e., those that are converted) The vast majority of educated and intelligent men and ladies and those capable of independent thought do consider them as forming part of the Parsi community.

Question.—According to you what would be the community at the time of birth of a posthumous child of a Parsi mother whose father is unknown ?

Answer.—Zoroastrian community.

Question.—Would it make a difference if in the case of a posthumous child the father was known to be an alien but the mother expressed and

Cross examination of NN Katrak, Trustee of the Anjuman Atash Behram of the priests of the Bhuggasarth Sect

Q) Since Mrs. Tata's case 'Parsis' have a well-defined settled definition?

A) The 'Panchayat case' had two issues. One was the validity of the trustees as Trustees. The second was whether an alien by conversion became entitled to the full rights and privileges of a Zoroastrian. The first issue was ruled out of order on the ground that the proper party was not the complainant. Hence the Panchayat case decided nothing in connection with that question.

Q) Does not judgment of Sir D Davar provide a well-settled definition of the 'Parsi Community'?

A) Certainly not, because that part of the judgment has no value.

Q) Among Parsis, what does the word 'Parsi' indicate at the present day?

A) Any person professing the Zoroastrian faith.

This was the view of the Bhuggasarth priests in 1915 recorded in court.

At this time, Justice Davar's *obiter dictum* expressed during the course of his judgment in 1908 in the Petit Vs Jeejeebhoy case was not accepted by the Parsis or by the Bhuggasarth priests of Navsari, who were ruled by the Gaekwad of Baroda.

PARSIS AND THE PRESS

The Kanga family had been the chroniclers of Calcutta's Zoroastrian and Gujarati population. Parsis were in the forefront as editors of many newspapers and the rivalry between the orthodox and reformist sections of society was being daily reported in the newspapers. They even created a cartoon character called 'Mr. Best Orthodox' and brought out many comic illustrations in the Hindi Punch. *Strangely, these cartoons, through their illustrations give a very explicit picture of what happened in the early 1900s.*

Edulji Navroji Kanga was born in a poor priestly family in Navsari. His mother's name was Kooverbai and father's name, Navroji. Having lost his father at an early age, he was sent to his father's friends in Bombay where he studied at Fort High School.

One of his relatives was a junior reporter in the *Bombay Gazette*. At his recommendation, Edulji joined a small press, on condition that he would only get a salary after he had learned the work. Later he got a job in the reporting department of the *Akbar-e-Soudagar* in Bombay.

In 1899, his father-in-law, Edulji Jamaspi Desai, who was working in Rallis India in Calcutta, died. The company appointed his son-in-law Edulji Kanga in their shipping department in Calcuta.

He served Rallis brothers for fourteen years and whilst in this service, he acted as the Calcutta correspondent of *Jam-e-Jamshed* and *Akbar-e-Soudagar,* sending news about Calcutta Parsis. He also contributed a regular column titled 'Letter from Calcutta'. This inspired him to start his own newspaper in Calcutta. He retired from Rallis brothers in November 1913 and started the Navroz Printing Works, the first Gujarati Press in Calcutta. In the beginning it was only a news sheet and was distributed free to those who spoke Gujarati in Calcutta.

On 25 December 1917 the fourth All India Bhatia Conference was held in Calcutta and on 26 December a meeting of the Indian National Congress was held under the Presidentship of Ms Annie Besant. Providing a full coverage of these events was the first issue of *Navroz* dated Saturday, 29 December 1917.

The *Navroz* was the only Gujarati weekly in eastern India. It became the chronicler of the Gujarati and Zoroastrian population of the region.

On 5 February 1955 Edulji passed away at the age of eighty-two and *Navroz* thrived under the joint editorship of his son Navel and his daughter-in-law Jaloo. Both have left for their heavenly abode and the Navroz Printing Works is also no more.

In 1914 leading Parsis in the world of journalism included the editor of *Hindi Punch*, Barjorjee Naoroji Apakhtyar; journalist RP Masani; *Jam-e-Jamshed* editor, JB Marzban, *Raast Goftar* editors, Kaikhasru Navrojee Kabrajee and Pallonji Burjorji Desai;

Edulji Navroji Kanga

Navel Kanga

Jaloo Navel Kanga

The arrival of Dastur Kaikobad in Rangoon from Poona to perform Bella's navjote. 'A comet,' Hindi Punch, 7 June 1914, p.19.

Sanj Vartaman editor, Rustom N Vatchaghandy; lawyer, journalist and editor of the Parsi almanac, *Parsi Prakash*, Rustam Barjorji Paymaster; *Oriental Review* editor RS Rustomji; Cawasji Temulji, who edited the *Poona Observer* and *Civil and Military Gazette*; *Sind Observer* editor, Dinsha Nanabhai Patel; *Akbar-e-Soudagar* editor, Byramji Bomanji Patel; *Gujarat Mitra* editor, Framji Kawasji Mehta; Feroz S Taleyarkhan, editor of the daily and weekly, *The Parsi; Parsi Sansar* editor, Rustomji Kharsedji Sidhwa; and Edulji Kanga of the Navroz Printing Works, Calcutta.

When the High Priest of the Deccan, Dastur Kaikobad Aderbad Dastur Noshirwan, visited Rangoon for Bella's navjote in 1914, other Parsis took advantage of his presence. It was a rare thing to have a Zoroastrian priest of his stature in Burma, and there was a backlog of ceremonies to be performed. Sapoorjee's wife (and Bella's adoptive mother) had her own navjote performed by Dastur Kaikobad Aderbad Dastur Noshirwan. She and Sapoorjee were then married by Dastur Kaikobad Aderbad Dastur Noshirwan, in a traditional Zoroastrian marriage ceremony.

Another Parsi family, the Contractors, performed the navjote ceremony of their son Behram.

Orthodox newspapers were acerbic in their coverage. In response there was litigation by the Contrators and Sapoorjee and those newspapers were sued. It was one of the most highly publicised Parsi libel episodes in the early twentieth century.

The case was covered under various lurid headlines: *The Rangoon Romance* and *Jam-e-Jamshed Defamation Case, Rangoon Defamation Case, Parsi Defamation Case, The Parsi Dispute.* The *Sanj Vartaman* went a step further titling their story *Bella and her half Burmese mother's Navjote and Marriage* written by Gustad Nariman. *Jam-e-Jamshed* newspaper lost the case and had to cover Sapoorjee's legal expenses, while two other newspapers, *Sanj Vartaman* and *Cherag,* apologised and withdrew their case.

"ZARTHOST-NO DISO, OOGHADO PETI NE KAHADO SISO"
"(Open the cupboard on the anniversary of Zoroaster's death and produce the bottle. –a Parsi proverb.)
Best Orthodox—What a sad day for me!
[Yesterday (19th June) was the anniversary of the death of Zoroaster. The Chief Presidency Magistrate delivered his judgment in the Jam-e Jamshed *defamation case, filed agaisnt the paper by the Zoroastrian Conference. The Magistrate convicted both the accused and fined the proprietor Mr. Jehangir B. Marzban Rs. 100 and the editor Mr. P. J. Marzban Rs. 600.]"*
[*Hindi Punch* (20 June 1915), 12.]

"OPEN INCENDIARISM"
"The Pharisee—Let us see if this best of purifiers won't cleanse my community!"
(A controversy is once more raging in the Parsi papers of Bombay over the admission of a girl into the Zoroastrian fold by the performance of the Navjot or the 'sacred thread-investiture ceremony by the learned high-priest of the Parsis in the Deccan,
Sardar Kiakobad Hosang, at Rangoon.)"
[*Hindi Punch* (12 April 1914), 10.]

"AN INKY SPORT!"
"Indulged in [by] some of the Bombay Parsi dailies morning and evening, to the digust of the sensible portion of the community."
[*Hindi Punch* (19 April 1914), 12.]

"VICTORIOUS!"
from "Chow-Chow: The Jame *and the Z. C."*
[*Hindi Punch* (27 June 1915), 14.]

The *Hindi Punch* printed cartoons during the course of the investigation. In the first cartoon Mr. Best Orthodox sat drinking and weeping (as the Orthodox lost the libel suit). They also printed cartoons on the Bella case unfurling in court.

Bella's navjote was performed in 1914 and the case Saklat Vs Bella was admitted in March 1915. Both the navjotes in Rangoon and the defamation cases against the newspapers were being covered extensively in the newspapers. It was common knowledge (maybe the most-talked-about event at that time) and the final judgment in the defamation case was given in July 1915.

Sapoorjee's libel case against the Marzbans of *Jam-e-Jamshed* lasted the longest. To begin with, *Jam-e-Jamshed* published two further articles that their lawyers held up as apologies. Sapoorjee's lawyer responded that these only aggravated the initial libel and proved malice. The Marzbans also published a public appeal for funds to cover the paper's legal costs for the suit. 'The Parsi Zoroastrian Defence Fund' was the brainchild of Dinshaw Davar, the Parsi Judge in the High Court of Bombay, who made the inaugural contribution of Rs 100. The fund increased the conflict, as did the support of Bombay-based reformist organisations who came out in support of Sapoorjee. The libel suit was finally settled on 20 August 1914.

The second libel case against *Jam-e-Jamshed* reached judgment in July 1915. Marzban was fined Rs 100 and his son Rs 600 *(Jam-e-Jamshed Defamation Case,* 4 July 1915).

The Trust Deed of the Late Ervad D.B. Mehta's Zoroastrian Anjuman Atash Adaran which appointed Dastur Kaikobad Aderbad Dastur Noshirwan, Head Priest of Calcutta, as the Calcutta Atash Adaran's spiritual guide in the observance of its religious rites, was dated September 1915.

The fact is that even in 1915 the Parsi Zoroastrians were puzzled about their identity. The orthodox view expressed by Justice Davar was observed by some. The reformist view of the learned priests like Dastur Kaikobad and Dastur Kaikhasru was followed by the educated and intelligent sections of society. In many ways, we were a community divided. Was Calcutta's Parsi Zoroastrian community reformist or orthodox?

The Cylopedia of India informs us that RD Mehta was a leader of the Parsi community and an exponent of its views.

The following facts reveal RD Mehta's views:

1. RD Mehta's family was the plaintiff in the Petit Vs Jeejeebhoy case. RD Tata had converted his wife, Susaune, to the Zoroastrian religion and now wanted her to be entitled to the benefits of the trusts and be allowed entry into the fire temple.
2. In 1915 when Bella's navjote had recently been performed and the libel cases were being extensively covered in the newspapers, RD Mehta selected Dastur Kaikobad Aderbad Dastur Noshirwan to consecrate the Atash Adaran made in memory of his father. He stipulated that Dastur Kaikobad should be followed in the observance of religious rites and practices at the Atash Adaran. He named Dastur Kaikobad as head priest of his Atash Adaran. In Schedule B of the Trust Deed of the Atash Adaran which had a list of prayers to be performed for his family, he included a monetary tribute to be sent to Dastur Kaikobad every year. This showed the tremendous respect he had for Dastur Kaikobad.
3. He selected Dastur Kaikhasru Jamaspjee to perform the Tana ceremony of the Tower of Silence.
4. The community in Calcutta was supportive of its priests. They respected them as Head Priests of the community and followed them for their religious guidance. There was no censure against them at any time. In fact Dastur Kaikobad was given the honour and respect of being selected as Head

FIGURE 9:
"I AM AN INDEPENDENT DASTUR."
from "The Rangoon Romance (Bella and the Anjuman)"
[*Hindi Punch* (7 June 1914), 14.]

'I am an independent Dastur': Dastur Kaikobad Aderbad Dastur Noshirwanji, High Priest of the Deccan

Priest of the newly established Late D.B. Mehta's Zoroastrian Anjuman Atash Adaran.

If these facts are to be taken into account and the past taken as a guide, then the way ahead is clear. Even a hundred years ago, our priests were very sure that the path to growth and harmony lay in accepting people from ouside the community into ours if they were sincere and they were willing to convert to the Zoroastrian cause.

But the past lies forgotten.

RD Mehta, his son and daughter-in-law were all lawyers. They used the words Parsi Zoroastrian in the Trust Deed of the Atash Adaran as they understood it and gave us a cue to remember and understand their views. They mentioned the name of the famous Dastur Kaikobad as the priest to be followed.

How was RD Mehta to know that his fearlessly independent Dastur Kaikobad Aderbad Dastur Noshirwan, who insisted on following his conscience in performing Bella's navjote and who was being constantly covered in the newspapers, would be completely forgotten a hundred years later?

I hope this book will help readers to step into the past and see the Calcutta community as it really was. And gather the courage to take difficult decisions even though they seem to be against the grain of lazy thinking within the community.

PARSI ZOROASTRIAN INSTITUTIONS OF CALCUTTA

Calcutta Zoroastrian Community's Religious & Charity Fund

In 1864 Parsis had been in Calcutta for over a hundred years and the population of the community in Calcutta was about 100. It was decided to form an Anjuman of the Parsis of Calcutta.

Prior to 1864, all the needs and affairs of the community were borne by the Banaji family. On 7 February 1864 a meeting was called under the Chairmanship of Maneckji Rustomji Banaji at the Banaji Atash Adaran. At this meeting, Sorabji Shapurji Bengalee said that so far Rustomji Cowasji Banaji and now his son, Maneckji Rustomji Banaji, have taken upon themselves the responsibility of the community, looked after the needy and borne all the expenses of the Anjuman's charities. Now that there were 100 Parsis in Calcutta and many well-to-do business houses, it was proper not to take advantage of one family and to form an Anjuman and a separate Religious & Charity Fund as in Bombay and elsewhere.

He suggested that the amount of Rs 2,500 collected for the fund should be handed over to the trustees elected at this meeting. He then presented the draft of the trust deed and everyone present voted for the formation of the 'Calcutta Zoroastrian Community's Religious & Charity Fund'. Maneckji Rustomji Banaji, Cowasji Pestonji Gora and Dhunjeebhoy Byramjee Mehta were the first three trustees elected.

The Original Deed of Trust was dated 31 October 1867 and the trustees in 1867 were Maneckji Rustomji Banaji, Cowasji Pestonji Gora and Nowrojee Pestonji Dhalla.

The books of the fund were handled by the firm of Dosabhai Framji Cama. Then a subscription list was circulated and Rs 7,123 was collected. In this list, the principal donations were Rs 1,255 from the Banaji family, Rs 1,251 from Behramji Cama, Rs 1,001 from Hormasji Bomanji Cama and Rs 1,001 from Dosabhai Framji Cama.

The Trust Deed reads:

> To all to whom these presents shall come, Maneckjee Rustomji of Chowringhee Road in the town of Calcutta Merchant, Cowasjee Pestonjee of Ezra Street in Calcutta aforesaid Merchant, and Nowrojee Pestonjee Dhalla of Ezra Street in Calcutta aforesaid Merchant, Member of the Zoroastrian Community commonly called in India Parsis send greetings.

A century later, with a substantial Parsi population in the city, and to meet the changing requirements of the community, it was felt that the Trust Deed needed some amendments and additions and the High Court of Calcutta on 04 September 1968 sanctioned certain amendments to the original Trust Deed. Till then, the trustees, once elected, held office for life. Under the amendments future trustees once elected could hold office for a period of seven years only, although they would be eligible for re-election and the number of trustees was also increased from three to five.

Some other additions were also sanctioned by the court clarifying the procedure for election of trustees, as well as their powers and duties.

The Trust manages and administers the following properties:

1. Manackjee Rustomjee Dharamsalla at 9, Bow Street (1909).
2. Khorshed Madan Mansion at 84, Lenin Sarani (1928) with twenty-five flats and four shops.

3. Property at 6, Grant Lane (1940) with ten flats.
4. Jamshedji Rustomji Saklat Ravangah (1934) and Navazbai Annexe at 1, Saklat Place (1954) with six flats.
5. The Tower of Silence (Dokhma) at Beliaghata which was first built in 1822 and the new one which was consecrated in 1912.
6. Property at 52, Chowringhee Road (1957) received as gift from the late Trustee Seth Edulji Shapurji Olpadvala which has a Community Hall which is available to the Parsis for various functions, meetings and community gatherings.

The Trust has been helping the community by providing assistance towards general welfare and also assistance for education, housing, medical care and entrepreneurship. The Trust also renders assistance to the various other Parsi institutions in Kolkata, such as:

1. The Calcutta Parsi Amateur Dramatic Club (1907)
2. The Calcutta Parsee Club (1908)
3. The Saklat Physical Culture Institute (1933)
4. The Parsi Zoroastrian Association (1935)
5. The Calcutta Zoroastrian Stree Mandal (1936)
6. The Calcutta Parsi Youth League (1939)

There are at present about 400 Parsis in Kolkata.

The Calcutta Parsi Youth League

Established in 1939, it was a splinter group of the Parsi Zoroastrian Association, since the founding fathers felt that the Association did not cater to the youth of the community. The organisation was formed with the intention of bonding with the youth of our community. The objectives of the League were to provide opportunities to young people to exchange views and opinions and share their talent with others via contests, discussions, debates, lectures and excursions, and to be of service to the Parsi community in general and Parsi youth in particular.

The Calcutta Parsi Amateur Dramatic Club

On 14 September 1907 a group of Parsi thespians banded together to form the club. In 1908 the club's maiden performance was in honour of the Calcutta Parsis on the occasion of Navroz, waiving its fees. This would continue for the next ninety-nine years and in August 2007 that magical century mark was ushered in. One hundred years of the *Natak* performed each and every year, come hell or high water.

In 1910 the club repeated its performance for the Gujarati-speaking communities and this too would become a tradition.

In the early and middle years of its existence, long serious plays, tragedies and melodramas, replete with a number of songs, were the order of the day. But with the passage of time, tastes changed and hilarious comedies sans songs took over. Another change was the presence of ladies on the stage 1955 onwards; prior to that males, properly made-up, played female roles.

The club derives its main revenue from advertisements in the brochures published at the time of the *Natak*, and donates part of its surplus funds to deserving charities.

To commemorate the memory of departed members, the club has established Educational Scholarship Funds dedicated to helping out needy Parsi students.

The Parsi Zoroastrian Association

This association was founded in 1935 to promote the religious, social, economic and intellectual activities of the Parsi community in Calcutta and to study and solve problems confronting the community. The founder members were the Late Dr DN Wadia, Head of the Geological Survey, the late CHM Rustomji and ES

Olpadvala (the latter two were trustees of the Calcutta Zoroastrian Community's Religious & Charity Fund as well). The first joint Hony. Secretaries were the late Mr KS Colah and the late MCH Rustomji. Mr JJ Modi was the first Hony. Treasurer and he continued to serve until he passed away in 1975. The members of the First Managing Committee included the late A Dinshaw, who was an active member as well as a joint secretary for many years and who played an important part in guiding the destiny of the Association. The other founder members were Mr SS Nazir, Mr RT Saklath and Dr JK Wadia. Mr RT Saklath passed away in March 1979, after serving this organisation for forty-four years in various capacities.

With the beginning of social gatherings for debates and lectures, the Parsi Zoroastrian Association developed into a study group inviting scholars of eminence in Bengal, Bombay and other places to address a select gathering on subjects such as philosophy, ancient history and religion. It has also helped impart religious instruction to children and held annual competitions giving silver medals and cash prizes.

The association has published many books which have been praised by scholars from different parts of the world. Of particular note are:

1. *The Hymns of Atharvan Zarathushtra* by JM Chatterjee
2. *Atharvan Zarathushtra, the Foremost Prophet* by JM Chatterjee
3. *The Message of the Gathas as Reflected by Masnavi* by JM Chatterjee
4. *The Gospel of Zarathushtra* by JM Chatterjee
5. *'Fravaranee for navjote-age children'*
6. *'Daily Prayers of the Zoroastrians'* (in English) by Framroz Rustomji
7. *Hymns of Ecstasy* by Cyrus S Meherji
8. *The Paradise Dweller* by Cyrus S Meherji
9. *Return of the Paradise Dweller* by Cyrus S Meherji

10. *The Flickering Flame* by Cyrus S Meherji
11. *I am Cyrus* by Cyrus S Meherji

The Saklat Physical Culture Institute

This institute was inaugurated on 1 July 1933 under the Chairmanship of Prof. DN Wadia. It is registered under the West Bengal Societies Registration Act 1961 and is temporarily located at 9, Bow Street, Kolkata 700 012.

Its aims and objectives are to encourage and develop the character and physical condition of the youth of the Parsi community through the following activities: gymnastics, swimming and scouting/guiding. Both the gymnasium and swimming sections which used to be very active in the past are now regrettably at a standstill. However since 1936 with the introduction of the Scouts and Guides section, the exciting world of scouting made a grand entry and is at present the main activity of the institute.

The Scout Troop, under the First Calcutta District Association of Bharat Scouts and Guides, was founded on 5 October 1936 under the leadership of Mr Ardeshir Kaikobad Batlivala and later on, to enable all children of the community to take full advantage of this worldwide movement, a Cub Pack was formed in July 1957 followed by a Bulbul Flock in April 1967 and a Guide Company in April 1968.

The institute has come a long way since then and has had to its credit hundreds of boys and girls who have grown into mature men and women holding important positions in their various fields of activities; together with leaders in the Scouting Guiding Movement who have held and are still holding posts at District and State levels.

In April 2009 the institute opened a new chapter in its history by becoming the first Kolkata Parsi Institute to welcome children whose mothers are Parsi Zoroastrians and whose fathers are non-Parsis, to become 'Associates' of the institute. Through a resolution passed by an overwhelming majority at an Extraordinary General

Meeting on 29 April 2009, the new rule came into effect. Thus the institute stood up for the cause of Parsi women and gave them an opportunity to virtually be at par and get equality of status in what was traditionally a male bastion.

The Calcutta Parsi Club

Five Parsi stalwarts established a cricket club on 4 November 1908. Over the years, the club expanded, not only in the size of its tent, but also in the number of its members and its sporting disciplines.

The first club tent was erected in 1908 on the Maidan, south of the present Mohammedan Sporting Club, and was shifted three times thereafter to different locations on the Maidan till it ended up at its present site on P-49 Guru Nanak Sarani (Mayo Road) in 1922. In 1974, the tent was last expanded on reconstruction and is now one of the largest on the Maidan, boasting of tennis courts which few others have.

The Parsi Club which started as a cricket club, continued as such for quite some time. In due course, the sporting activities were extended to football, hockey, tennis, basketball, badminton, table tennis, billiards, carroms and athletics.

The club's membership now stands at over 600 and includes a number of outstation members, both in and outside India. Initially, membership was restricted to males but in 1932 ladies were admitted and it is they who have really done the club proud. Many of the male and female members have proudly represented the state and country.

The Calcutta Zoroastrian Stree Mandal

This organization was founded in 1936 with the principal objective of granting relief to indigent families of our community residing in and around Calcutta and to assist them in improving their condition.

The Mandal extends help in the form of medicine, medical care, hospitalisation, rations, supplementary diet, school and college education fees, including cost of books, clothes, etc. All cases are reinvestigated annually.

In 1967 a two-storeyed building in Park Circus was acquired through the generous and active support of the Parsi community of Calcutta and efforts in raising funds through various programmes. In 1980 another floor was added. At present the building houses nine needy Parsi families.

The Mandal is affiliated to Women's Co-ordinating Council, West Bengal and West Bengal Council of Women. Through these organizations the Mandal sponsors adult literacy programmes, education and vocational training of girls in poor villages of West Bengal. The education fees of one child are paid to the SOS Children's Village, West Bengal. Donations are made to appropriate funds in times of natural calamities and to other deserving causes like the Leprosy Mission, orphanages, infirmaries, etc., in Gujarat and West Bengal.

The Mandal has nearly 300 members comprising Life, Ordinary and Associate members. Donations and subscriptions help the Mandal to serve the needy. All donations made to the Mandal are exempt under Section 80G of the Income Tax Act, 1961.

The members' monthly social programmes are varied, cultural and entertaining. They provide an opportunity for members to get together and thereby help to augment the funds.

APPENDIX I

Archival Letters and Press Cuttings

19 January 1885
R.D. Mehta to Dadabhai Naoroji, telegraph
Calcutta
M-100
In Unpublished Patwardhan Vol. 1, IMG 1036
One page, telegraph slip
Original: brittle and broken into pieces.

INDIAN TELEGRAPH.

To (Station)	From (Station)
Bombay	Calcutta

Words.	Day.	Hour.	Minute
23/2	19	18	8

TO (Person)	FROM (Person)
Dadabhoi [sic] Naoroji Esq 16 Marine Street fort [sic]	R.D. Mehta

What would you recommend native community to do here for lord Randolph.

BOMBAY 19-1-85

21 January 1885
Dadabhai Naoroji to Rustomji D. Mehta
Bombay
N-1 (218)
In Unpublished Patwardhan Vol. 1, IMG 1036
Three handwritten pages on tissue copy paper.
Illegible in parts: due to blurriness. Ink has dissolved paper in places. Brittle.
Photographed

5th Khetwady Lane
Bombay 21st Jan 1885

My dear Rustomji

Your telegram came to hand late in the evening when I returned home.

Till Lord Randolph was here, he was unwilling to meet in a publish meeting or to give any public address. We had only a conference at Mr Behramji Malbari's house, of which a report has appeared in the papers. If you can get Lord R to attend or address a public meeting, you may do so. If not, if he be still of the same mind as here, it would be better to have a private conference with him of all or a good many of your best social reformers, who know their own subjects very well [?]. For you will find Lord R putting you questions which will floor you, if you are not well up in what you say, and are not well able to support with facts and proofs. Mere random talk and hits will not do with him.

Perhaps a private conference like this with free conversation and interchange of ideas will be more useful and effective than a public address by him or by others. It is very desirable that a person like him should return to England with some definite clear notions of our most important wants. I have given him a copy of my "Poverty of India" and Condition of Inida. And a written memorandum of the most important political reforms, viz, simultaneous examinations for all the Services (excepting Military) in England and India as the principal remedy for the material and moral poverty of India. If Bengal also could impress upon him this first most essential reform it will be a great gain. For the uncovenanted services, I have urged that a system like that of England of examinations for all the different departments of the State by the Civil Service Commissioners should be introduced here, so that there will be a fair field for Natives and Europeans alike, and each department will get servants most fitted for it by their idiosyncrasies and special preparation.

Such a course of free and personal conversation should be adopted with every Englishman of note that may visit India. The next most important reform is that of having representative, elected, non-official members in the Legislative Councils instead of nominated members. If we have these two reforms, simultaneous examinations and representation in the Councils, we shall have opened up a clear and hopeful course, for both our material and moral, and political progress.

Yours truly
Dadabhai Naoroji

29 January 1885
Rustomji D. Mehta to Dadabhai Naoroji
Calcutta
M-100 (1)
Two handwritten pages
Original: brittle

D.B. MEHTA & Co.
CALCUTTA.

55, Canning Street
29th January 1885

My dear Sett Dadabhai

You will kindly accept my most sincere thanks for your favor of the 21st instant. I had circulated your letter amongst a number of my friends who I assure you have read with intense pleasure & interest. We are organising an Evening Party at the India Club for Lord Randolph & have telegraphed for his consent. No reply is yet received but there is no fear of his refusing the invitation. An attempt is also made to secure a private interview with him. Do you think we might impress on Lord R's mind the desirability of admitting natives to the Commissioned ranks of the Military Service? If I could be of any use to you here I would indeed be very glad. Some time ago you wrote to me 2 or 3 letters in connection with the "Voice of India" & I was extremely sorry for not replying to them, & I am sure you will excuse me when I tell you that my father was very sick at the time, in fact his condition was most precarious, & owing to that cause I was not in a fit state of mind to attend to any business. Mr. Hume has written a letter to Narendra Nath Sen & the question of establishing telegraphic service with England weekly is on the carpet. What do you think of Lal Mohun Ghose's candidature for the Parliament? I sincerely wish that he gets in, he or any one from India if once gets in the Parliament then I think the time has fairly come for India to raise a hue & cry for having representative ~~parliaments~~ Councils. The matter then should be agitated thro' the length & breadth of India & not allowed to drop till we have gained our points.

With my best wishes for your health & happiness.

Believe me
Ever Yours Sincerely
R.D. Mehta

Dadabhai Naoroji Esq.

5th Khetwady Lane—Bombay

Lal Mohun is a good speaker no doubt, but he lacks in figures & unless he makes that his special study he will not be very successful.

5 March 1885
R.D. Mehta to Dadabhai Naoroji
Calcutta
M-100 (2)
Two handwritten pages
Original: brittle.

THE EMPRESS OF INDIA COTTON MILLS Co. Ld. CALCUTTA. [seal]
55, Canning Street,
Calcutta, 5th March 1885

My dear Mr. Dadabhai

I owe you apologies for not having sooner answered your very kind letter. Lord Randolph beyond visiting Sir Jotindro Mohun Tagore at his private residence did not accept anybody's invitation nor did he grant any interview. But from the little we saw of him we found him to be a man full of information upon almost every topic. We expect Mr. Hume here shortly. He will be the guest of Mr. Nundmohun Ghose,—Lallmohun's Brother. It is the intention of our Bengalee Friends to establish a weekly or fortnightly telegraphic service between here & England independently of Bombay, & with that in view they have I think succeeded in securing some Rs. 20.000. It is a great pity that our aristocratic class remain quite aloof from the Reformed Party, & do not give their desired support. Our Lieutenant Governor seems to enjoy their confidence & his advice they act upon. The public utterances of our Governor are beyond all question hostile to the native community & in spite thereof I cannot understand why our rich Zemindars should cling to him. The Europeans are beginning to dislike our present Viceroy who they fear is more for the Natives than for his own class. I am afraid he will retire with the change of the Ministry.

Enclosed please find my subscription—No. M68 55013 Bombay 1st August 1881 for Rs. 10—to the Voice of India for the Current Year.

Trusting you are keeping good health & with kindest regards

I am, Yours Sincerely
R.D. Mehta

How is your son Ardesir? Has he got over that defect in the leg?

To Dadabhai Naoroji Esq.
Ketwady [sic] 5th Lane
Bombay.

19 September 1885
Rustomji D. Mehta to Dadabhai Naoroji
Bombay
N-1 (353)
One handwritten page on tissue copy paper
Original: brittle. Text is extremely faint.

Bombay 19th September 1885.

My dear Rustamjee

I have received your kind telegram and thank you very much for the good wishes and congratulations you have sent me

Wishing you a happy New Year

Your's truly
Dadabhai Naoroji

R.D. Mehta Esq
Calcutta.

20 July 1886
Behramji M. Malabari to Dadabhai Naoroji
Fort, Bombay
M-32 (100)
Four handwritten pages
Original: brittle
Photographed

Office of the Indian Spectator,
24, HORNBY ROAD, FORT,
Bombay, July 20 1886

Dear Dad:

[...]

Mr Mehta from Calcutta was writing the other day [?] to ask if we cd raise a fund for you. I asked him to wait till you are consulted. If a call is not well responded to it wd be bad.

[...]

So after all, I hope our friends here may admit tthat yr going has turned out more useful than yr not going.

Yours truly
BM Malabari

10 September 1886
Dadabhai Naoroji to Rustomji D. Mehta
National Liberal Club, London
N-1 (639)
One handwritten page on tissue copy paper
Original: brittle. Text is very blurry.

National Liberal Club
London 10th September 1886

My dear Rustamjee

I inclose a letter for the Secretaries of the British Indian and National Indian Associations, requesting them to distribute some copies of Mr S. Smith[1] MP's pamphlets

Kindly hand the letters to them with my compliments. Hope you are quite well

Your's truly
Dadabhai Naoroji

R.D. Mehta Esq
Calcutta

1 Samuel Smith?

25 August 1887
Dadabhai Naoroji to Rustomji D. Mehta
National Liberal Club, London
N-1 (93)
Two handwritten pages on tissue copy paper
Original: preserved in wax paper. Blurry and faint.

National Liberal Club
London 25th August 1887

Dear Rustamjee

I have given letters of introduction to Mr W.S. Caine, M.P. for Sir Jotindro Mohan Tagore, Mr Rajandralal, Hon [?] Peary Mohan Mukerji, Mr Surendranath Bannerji, Babu Narendra Nath Sen, Mr W.C. Bonnerjee and yourself. I hope you may be able to give him what attention you can, and let our other friends know that I have given letters for them. It is very important that MPs should visit India, and we should help them as well as we can to learn the true state of affairs in India, our [?] wants &c. Mr Henry Norman of the Pall Mall Gazette also is going to visit India. He will arrive in India, via America & China, around [?] January. Him also I have given letters to the same friends mentioned above. Give [?] him what attention you can. He is a well wisher of the Natives, and if he is helped to understand India correctly, it will be a great gain to India in the public journalism here

You may receive some letters addressed to him in your care, which keep and give to him on his arrival at Calcutta. Give my kind regards to all the friends whom are so kind to me and to your father & all others [?]

Your's truly
Dadabhai Naoroji

R.D. Mehta Esq
55 Canning St
Calcutta.

20 October 1887
Dadabhai Naoroji to Rustomji D. Mehta
London
N-1 (827)
One handwritten page on tissue copy paper
Original: brittle and frayed. Writing is extremely blurry.

London 20th October 1887

My dear Rustamjee

I have given to Sir [Thomas] Fowell Buxton, a leading Philanthropist of England letters of introduction as below

Sir Jotindro Mohun Tagore
Mr Rajedralal
Narendranath Sen
Hon Peary Mohan Mookerjee
Pandit Ishwar Chandra Videasagar
W.C. Bonnerjee
and yourself.

You will inform our friends and [...] to give such attention as you can to Sir Fowell.

I should like to know whether our friends have any objections to my giving such letters, when I am asked.

[...] Sir Fowell goes to Bombay by the [?] mail

Your's truly
Dadabhai Naoroji

R.D. Mehta
Calcutta.

8 June 1891
R.D. Mehta to Dadabhai Naoroji
Notting Hill, London
M-100 (3)
Two handwritten pages
Original: fair

[Seal:] R D M A CLEAR CONSCIENCE IS A SURE DEFENCE
~~55, CANNING STREET,~~
~~CALCUTTA.~~
23, Ladbroke Crescent
Notthing Hill W
June 8th/91

Dear Mr. Dadabhai

I have just received a letter from the Secy. N.L. club informing of my election as a Temporary Member of the club for which you will please accept my thanks. If you would kindly propose me as an Ordinary Member I would be obliged.

I would like to see you on Wednesday the 10th & would be glad to know your time

Yours very Sincerely
R.D. Mehta

Dadabhai Naoroji Esq.
National Liberal Club

~~Is it necessary for me to write to the Secy.~~
I have written to the Secy. Acknowledging receipt of his letter.

5 June 1900
R.D. Mehta to Dadabhai Naoroji
London
M-100 (4)

HOTEL MÉTROPOLE,
LONDON, W.C. June 5th 1900

My dear Mr Dadabhai

Many thanks for your note and enclosure. I have been elected a temporary member of the club just now for two months and do not wish to be elected a permanent member just yet as I am going away from London in a fortnight's time and do not know when I would be coming back if at all to London. In case I wish to be elected permanently I will send you the form sent by you duly filled up as desired. I hope you are keeping in good health. I was pleased to see you looking so well the other day I called on you.

With my best thanks I am
Yours Sincerely
RD [illegible?]

24 May 1891
R.D. Mehta to Dadabhai Naoroji
Naples, Italy
M-100 (5)
Two handwritten pages
Original: fair

[Seal:] R D M A CLEAR CONSCIENCE IS A SURE DEFENCE
55, CANNING STREET,
CALCUTTA.

B.I.S.N. Co's.
S.S. "India"
Naples May 24th/91

Dear Seth Dadabhai

I am on my way to England with my 2 sons whom I wish to bring up for the Civil Service; our friend Mr. Manmohan Ghose has written to his son to make all arrangements & I hope to receive a letter from him at Plymouth. We will D.V. [?] reach London, Albert Docks, on the 2nd or 3rd June & if you would kindly enroll me as an Hony. Member of either Northbrook or the National Liberal Club I would feel greatly obliged. My stay in England will not extend more than 3 or 4 months & during that time I shall be travelling at [sic] difference places,—Scotland & Lancashire. Where could I meet you in London? A reply in the care of the Agents Messrs. Weekes Phillips & Co., Plymouth will reach me properly

Trusting this will find you in perfect health.

Yours very sincly,
R.D. Mehta

Dadabhai Naoroji Esq.
National Liberal Club
London.

12 July 1892
R.D. Mehta to Dadabhai Naoroji
Calcutta
M-100 (6)
Three handwritten pages
Original: fair.

[DN:] Answer
20.8.92

[Seal:] R D M A CLEAR CONSCIENCE IS A SURE DEFENCE
55, CANNING STREET,
CALCUTTA.

My dear Sethjee Dadabhai

Every individual member of our family write with me in offering you our very warmest congratulations on your Election & return to Parliament. The whole of India feels pleased & proud on this wonderful & unprecedented achievement. We contemplate holding a public meeting & transmitting therefrom a cablegram of thanks to the Electors of Finsbury. But we are now waiting for the result of the Scrutiny demanded by your opponent Captn. Penton. We look forward to that with very great anxiety [and] sincerely pray that it may result in your favor. If I could be of any use to you in Calcutta pray let me know. Trusting you are in enjoyment of perfect health & with every good wish for you

I am
Yours very Sincly
R.D. Mehta

24 September 1906
R.D. Mehta to Dadabhai Naoroji
Calcutta
M-100 (7)
Two handwritten pages
Original: fair

[DN:] replied
25/10/1906

[Seal:] R D M A CLEAR CONSCIENCE IS A SURE DEFENCE
55, CANNING STREET,
CALCUTTA.
24th Septr. 1906

My dear Seth Dadabhai

We are pleased to learn that you have accepted the Presidentship of this year's Congress. The Bengalees are fighting among themselves & any one & every one poses as a Leader. In the lot we have some very good men & some self seeking. I am sure your presence would tend to settle the matter down smoothly. We will take it as a great favor if you will put up with us as you so very kindly did on your last visit. Pray accept this as an invitation from my dear old parents & all of us. We would not say how very pleased we would be to put you up and to show you your likeness gracing and ornamenting our agiary.

By last mail I have sent my fifth son Khusroo for medical tuition with his eldest brother Maneck, the barrister whom I dare say you know. My barrister son Maneck aspires to a Judgeship of an High Court & I have to solicit your kind help in the matter. Need I say how grateful we all would be by our helping him & putting him in the way.

I sincerely trust you are keeping well & with our united kindest regards & best wishes,

I am,
Yours Sincerely,
R.D. Mehta

15 March 1886
Henry J.S. Cotton to Dadabhai Naoroji
Calcutta
C-266
In Unpublished Patwardhan Vol. 1, IMG 447-48
Four handwritten pages
Original: brittle and broken

March 15th 1886.

3 Kyd Street
Calcutta.

My dear Sir,

I have been asked by our mutual friend Mr. R.D. Mehta to write to you and I hope you will therefore excuse the liberty I take in so doing. But it is very important I think that those who take a similar and equal interest in public affairs should not hesitate to place themselves in communication with one another. You will have known something of me from my book: I have long known of you from your evidence in England, your published utterances and general reputation.

You will allow me to say that I hope you will be able to give evidence before this Parliamentary Commission. What we want is men with full knowledge of facts; in this respect, on the Bengal side in particular, Indian gentlemen are [...] deficient. Two or three of the best men from each Presidency should be deputed home: that it will be enough: but there ought to be a thoroughly organised agitation in this country so as to indicate as clearly as possible that the delegates are really representative. Meetings at every town in each Presidency should be held to make this quite clear.

I don't advocate the deputation of a few Members to examine witnesses in India: of course there is much to be said in favour of the purpose: but the preponderance of argument is agt. it. These members will be put up at Govt. House or by Mr. Justice Cunningham &c. and the indirect influences they will then be subjected to, morning, noon & night, will more than outweigh the value of any direct evidence they may record. Besides if any Members were deputed to India they would perhaps be Sir R. Temple, R. Lethbridge and L. Pelly!!

I hope I shall see you here at the Annual Conference next year. These conferences are producing a marked influence which will become greater every year.

If you find time to write me a line I shall be very pleased to get it

Yours sincerely
H.J.S. Cotton.

The
Honble Dadabhoy Naorojee.

25 July 1892

Byramjee R.D. Mehta to Dadabhai Naoroji
Upper Norwood, London
M-91
Two handwritten pages
Original: fair

"Bankside"
Lunham Road
Upper Norwood
S.E.

July 25th 1892.

My dear Sir,

I felt very happy & proud to learn from the papers some time ago about your successful attempt to enter Parlt. I send this to say that you have my very best wishes for similar successes in yourcareer as an M.P.

I am very sorry to say that I could not do myself the pleasure of waiting upon you, last Saturday, as on that day, in the afternoon I had to go to the University of London to enquire about the result of the Matriculation Examination for which I was a candidate. The result brought me to such a very deep grief that instead of doing my duty in attending you I came home and contended myself by reading the description of the dinner & speeches in this mornings papers.

I hope that in this season of joy and pride of the Indian people you will excuse this shortcoming on my part and in taking the liberty of writing to you

With very best wishes

I am

Dear Sir,

Very faithfully Yours

Byramjee R.D. Mehta

THE POLICE COURTS: THE VICE-CONSULAR DEFAMATION CASE
The Times of India (1861-current); Nov 21, 1900;
ProQuest Historical Newspapers: The Times of India (1838-2002)
pg. 3

THE POLICE COURTS.

THE VICE-CONSULAR DEFAMATION CASE.

At the Esplanade Police Court, yesterday, Mr. J Sanders Slater continued his inquiry into the case in which Mr. Cowasjee D. Rustomjee, Vice-Consul for Persia, charged Jallaludin Hoosein, proprietor and publisher of *Hablul Matin*, a weekly Persian newspaper published in Calcutta, with defamation.

Mr. F. Sorabjee Talyarkhan. barrister-at-law, instructed by Messrs. Smetham, Bland, and Noble, solicitors, appeared for the complainant; while Mr. W. R. Hamilton, barrister-at-law, instructed by Mr. Mirza Hoosein Khan, solicitor defended the accused.

The case for the defence having been closed, evidence was called by Mr Talyarkhan in rebuttal of the statements made by the witnesses called on behalf of the accused.

Mr. Cowasjee, the complainant, further examined by Mr. Talyarkhan, denied having ever urged Mr. R. D. Mehta to accept the Persian Consulship at Calcutta. He never told Mr. Mehta that he would have to spend five or six thousand rupees for getting the position. On the contrary whenever the witness went to Calcutta since 18?8 Mr. Mehta asked him to use his influence in getting his cousin, Mr. Hirjibhoy, removed from the post of Persian Consul at Calcutta, and to recommend his (Mr. Mehta's) name to the late Persian Consul-General. In return for this Mr. Mehta offered to pay Rs. 6,000 to Rs. 8,000 to the Consul-General, and make a very handsome present to the witness himself. The witness always refused to accede to the offer. Mr. Mehta was his bitterest enemy. The witness also denied having received any pecuniary help from Maharajah Tagore for getting him the Vice-Consulship at Calcutta. The witness knew that Mr. Mehta had given the Consul-General a phaeton costing about Rs. 1,600 as a present only after ten days' acquaintance. It was not true, as stated by Mr. Mehta, that the present was made at the witness's suggestion.

Further hearing of the case was adjourned.

Congratulations on the Victories
OUR OWN CORRESPONDENT
The Times of India (1861-current); Mar 6, 1900;
ProQuest Historical Newspapers: The Times of India (1838-2002)
pg. 5

Congratulations on the Victories.

(FROM OUR OWN CORRESPONDENT.)

CALCUTTA, MARCH 4.

The Committee of the Bengal Chamber of Commerce telegraphed on Saturday last to Sir George White, conveying the hearty congratulations of the members of the Chamber on his gallant and successful defence of Ladysmith. They also despatched a further telegram to Field Marshal Lord Roberts, conveying the hearty congratulations of the members of the Chamber on his Lordship's brilliant successes in South Africa.

Mr. R. D. Mehta, Consul for Persia, addressed the following letter of congratulation to H. E. the Viceroy :—" My Lord,—Allow me, as the representative of his Majesty the Shah of Persia in Calcutta, to offer my sincere congratulatious to her Most Gracious Majesty's Government on the glorious success that has attended the British arms in South Africa. Allow me also to express the hope that the victory that has been scored by Field Marshal Lord Roberts will lead to a speedy and successful termination of the war, and that British supremacy will be established once for all in South Africa."

The following reply was received by him :—" Sir,—I am directed by his Excellency the Viceroy to acknowledge the receipt of your letter, and to thank you cordially for your congratulations on the victory that has been achieved in South Africa by his Excellency Field Marshal Lord Roberts."—S. W. Lawrence, Private Secretary to H. E. the Viceroy.

In addition to communicating with H. E. the Viceroy, Mr. Mehta also cabled a congratulatory message. direct to Lord Roberts at Paardeberg as follows :—" From R. D. Mehta, Calcutta,—Accept sincerest congratulations on your most famous victory." The following reply was received from Lord Roberts :—" Osfontein, to R. D. Mehta, Calcutta, Many thanks for your kind congratulations."

Lord Roberts has replied to Sir William Lockhart's telegram of congratulation, as follows :—" I am much gratified and encouraged by your Excellency's telegram, and beg you to accept yourself and to convey to the Army of India my sincerest thanks for your kind congratulations."

CONSULAR DEFAMATION CASE.

On the Appellate Side of the High Court, the Hon. Mr. Justice Fulton and the Hon. Mr. Justice Batty disposed of the application made by Mr. Hamilton, instructed by Mr. M. H. Khan, on behalf of Jalaladin Hoosein, an accused in a case pending before the Chief Presidency Magistrate, Bombay. The accused applied for revision of the order passed by the Magistrate, on the 19th instant, refusing his application for the issue of a commission for the examination of witnesses at Calcutta. The accused is charged before the Magistrate with alleged defamation of Mr. Cowasji Dadabhoy, lately the Vice-Consul for Persia in Bombay.

The order appealed from was as follows:—In applications such as this, it is laid down by the Code that the circumstances of the case must be considered. As foreshadowed by Mr. Hamilton, the defence wishes to call ten witnesses who are to contradict the complainant flatly, and it appears to me extremely undesirable to have one witness personally before me; and the evidence of ten witnesses, on the opposite side, taken on commission. Still if this seems necessary for the ends of justice, I should consider whether the expense of bringing the witnesses from Calcutta is unreasonable or not. It is necessary to remember in connection with this point that this paper is a Calcutta paper, and that it goes so far afield as to hold up to public obloquy a man in Bombay. Any Calcutta editor who does such a thing does it with the presumed knowledge that he may be called upon to appear and to make good his defence in Bombay, and though it would cost a considerable amount of expense to bring the witnesses from Calcutta, it would also entail considerable expense on the complainant to be compelled to go to Calcutta to carry on his case there. I am at present extremely disinclined to order any commission to issue, but it appears to me that, as these Calcutta charges are not the only imputations that have been cast upon the complainant to-day, it would be advisable to postpone any actual order in the matter till the accused has had the opportunity of proving the local charges, viz, that the complainant has been masquerading in an Order bought for Rs. 25 in the Bombay bazaar, that he never received a firman from the Persian Government, and that he has fraudulently misappropriated a picture, the property of the Persian Consulate. It would be as well that these local questions should be disposed of first; and I adjourn the case for that purpose.

In a subsequent order, the Magistrate said: On the 29th May last, on Mr. Hamilton's application for a commission to issue for the examination of ten witnesses in Calcutta, I considered it advisable to postpone any ruling on the application until it had appeared how the local evidence had left the case. That local evidence has now been taken, and the application is renewed on this occasion for the examination of seven witnesses, or perhaps only four. For the reasons which I then gave, I stated that I was extremely disinclined to grant a commission. I will not repeat those reasons now, but I will only state that, in my opinion, the further development of the case has only confirmed me in the opinion I then formed, and I believe that it is absolutely necessary for the disposal of this case that I should have the witnesses before me personally. I regret that this should appear to lay a heavy burden of expense upon the accused, as I should also regret to lay a heavy burden upon the complainant, but I see no other course open to me than to require the attendance of all the accused's witnesses before myself, if I am to come to a satisfactory termination of this case. I must, therefore, refuse Mr. Hamilton's application.

Before their Lordships it was urged on behalf of the accused that the expenses of bringing the accused's witnesses to Bombay would amount to about Rs. 1,500; that this expense would be unreasonable under the circumstances of the case; and that the expenses of the complainant going to Calcutta would be small in comparison. Nor was it absolutely necessary that he should go there; but the witnesses might be examined by interrogatories and cross-interrogatories, which might be settled in Bombay. The issues to be tried at Calcutta were simple issues, which are suitable for enquiry by commission, and did not conflict in any way with the issues, of which evidence had already been given in Bombay. It was not essential that the Magistrate should examine personally the witnesses now at Calcutta. The applicant is a poor man. The inconvenience to the witnesses should be considered, and it would be unreasonable to require prominent persons, such as Mr. R. D. Mehta, C.I.E., and Raja Sir Sarendra Mohun Tagore to abandon their own business and journey to Bombay to give their evidence.

Their Lordships, on a consideration of all the circumstances of the case, rejected the application.

MORE PERSIAN TROUBLE.

ALLAHABAD, May 18.

The *Pioneer's* frontier correspondent states: Afghan officials in the districts to the south of the Oxus are having some trouble with traders from Russian territory who persist in entering the country. They are mostly disguised as Uzbegs, though some assume the garb of pilgrims on their way to Mecca from Central Asia. A number of them were lately arrested at Tashkurgan and Indarab and under orders from Kabul they are to be sent back across the Oxus. It is reported also that traders from Merv have lately tried to enter the Herat province, but without success.

Mohmand Malik, named Bazwan Khan, raided one of the Afghan road posts near Dakka last week. The post was burned and several persons were carried off. The reason for the raid is said to be that Bazwan Khan has been excluded from the list of Mohmand headmen to whom allowances are granted by the Amir.

MORE TROUBLE WITH OUTLAWS.

ALLAHABAD, May 17.

The outlaws who have taken up their residence in Afghanistan have lately been showing activity on the east of the Durand line. It appears that the Amir in pursuance of his agreement with the Government of India, issued fresh orders in March that such outlaws must move inland at least fifty miles from the Afghan border. The right of asylum was not to be denied to them, but they were warned that they must cease from raiding. It is, however, found impossible to enforce order in Khost, where the local tribesmen are still not under full control, and hence there are gangs which are still giving trouble in the borderland of the North-west Frontier Province, and the only way to deal with them is to hunt them down whenever they appear in British territory.

COTTON MILL LIQUIDATION.

CALCUTTA, May 17.

At a meeting to be held on the 25th instant, a resolution will be proposed to wind up the Empress of India Cotton Mills Co., whose factory was destroyed by fire some eighteen months ago. Messrs. R. D. Mehta, M. R. Mehta and C. P. Guzdar are appointed liquidators. Another resolution will move that Mr. R. D. Mehta, agent for life, will receive as compensation half a lakh of rupees and the agent's bungalow at the mill.

A COLONEL'S MISHAP.

SIMLA, May 17.

There will be a very large circle of friends of Colonel Deare, 8th Hussars, who will hear with great regret of a serious operation he has undergone. Early in the year he got a slight cut in his foot which obstinately got worse and finally the Colonel was sent from hospital at Lucknow to Kasauli, where it was eventually considered necessary to amputate his foot.

FIRE TEMPLE FOR CALCUTTA
The Times of India (1861-current); Sep 18, 1911;
ProQuest Historical Newspapers: The Times of India (1838-2002)
pg. 7

FIRE TEMPLE FOR CALCUTTA.

CALCUTTA, September 17.

The foundation-stone of a Parsi Fire Temple was laid at Metcalfe Street, Calcutta by Mrs. D. B. Mehta, on Sunday. About 20 years ago the late Mr. D. B. Mehta established a temple near his residence and at his own expense brought priests from Bombay. They came on foot from Bombay to Calcutta carrying with them the sacred fire. These were the first priests established in the Calcutta family of the late Mr. D. B. Mehta, and in order to perpetuate his name it was decided to make over the temple to the public.

It is reported that the epidemic of cholera at Mecca and Medina will eventually check the pilgrims from India.

Lieutenant J. J. Astor [illegible]

Parsees on the other. Regarding the latter the name that stands out most prominently is that of Sir Jamsetjee Jeejeebhoy, the recognized head of the Parsees of India. A splendid example of energy and enterprise—qualities that are, indeed, typical of the Parsees—the Jeejeebhoy family is of the humblest origin. A century ago, when the British Empire in India was being formed out of the crumbling ruins of the Mogul and the Mahratta, and all India was in chaos, the ancestor of the Jeejeebhoys was a poor lad, striving to gain his daily bread by the sweat of his brow.

Then, no sooner were modern methods of economics introduced into the country than this humble lad forthwith dreamt of millions. He started in business as a small merchant. So far the entire foreign trade of India has been in English hands—those of the East India Company. Now, for the first time, an Eastern entered the field.

In the absence of competition on the part of the conservative Hindus he increased his business, prospered, and finally amassed a fortune of £2,000,000. For his purpose India was a virgin soil, a new country as yet unexploited by modern methods—even as was the United States a generation ago; the cause of his success the same as that of the first American millionaires.

INDIA'S FIRST BARONET.

Because of his splendid munificence he was created first a K. C. B. and then a Baronet—the first in India. For, if he amassed a fortune, he knew how to spend it. He gave away a million pounds, half his fortune, in charities. Hospitals, colleges, and rest-houses were founded and endowed by him.

The present baronet, Sir Jamsetjee Jeejeebhoy, the third from the founder, succeeded in 1877, and since then has well maintained the traditions of his house. With increasing wealth he has increased the aim and purpose of his philanthropy. And no better proof could be given of the appreciation and gratitude of his countrymen than the general delight with which his selection to represent Bombay at the recent coronation was received by all its citizens.

Hardly less conspicuous is the Petit family. Even as the Jeejeebhoys made their fortunes in foreign trade, the Petits made theirs in cotton spinning. Half a century ago the first cotton mill in Bombay was founded by a Parsee—the late Cowasjee Nanabhoy Davar. Though confining himself solely to the spinning of yarns, he succeeded in accumulating considerable wealth.

Then the Petits went one better, for in 1855 Mr. Dinshaw Manockjee Petit erected the Oriental Spinning and Weaving Mill, which not only spun yarns, but wove cloth. This venture was so great a success that in 1860 Mr. Dinshaw was induced to erect another mill, the Manockjee Petit Spinning and Weaving Mill, thus named in memory of his father. The investment proved so profitable that several cotton mills were started by Mr. Dinshaw, one after another in rapid succession. Speedily he became the largest shareholder in the six leading cotton mills of Bombay—the Manockjee Petit Mill, the Dinshaw Petit Mill, the Victoria, the Mazagon, the Framjee Petit, and the Gordon Mills.

Besides spinning and weaving, Mr. Dinshaw also directed his attention to the manufacture of thread, hosiery, and fancy goods and to the dyeing of yarns.

FROM LANCASHIRE TO BOMBAY.

At the present day many cotton mills are working in Bombay, and more will soon be started. Already the entire yarn supply of India, and to some extent of China and Japan, is furnished by the Bombay mills. No doubt these yarns are now of the coarser kind, but the day must come when the Bombay factories will also learn to spin yarns of the highest "count." Then the sceptre of the Eastern trade in cotton cloth must pass from Lancashire to Bombay. And all due to the energy, the foresight, the enterprise of Dinshaw Manockjee Petit.

For his splendid philanthrophy, rivaling that of Sir Jamsetjee Jeejeebhoy, he, too, was made a Baronet in 1890. And now, both by marriage and by commercial partnership, the Petit family is closely allied with those of the other Parsee millionaires of India—the Wadias, the Readymoneys, the Camas. Mr. Nowrojee Manockji Wadia, whose recent gift of a million pounds to charity has been already mentioned, is the foremost of these.

These represent Parsee enterprise on the western side of India; on the eastern it is no less singular. The two great modern industries of India are cotton and jute. The Petits and the Wadias had captured the cotton on the Bombay side. It remained for the Mehtas to cross over to the Bengal side and capture the jute.

One would have imagined that the Tagores, the great Hindu family of Bengal (whose heir, the Maharajah Kumar Tagore, was here for the coronation as the representative of Calcutta), would not have permitted this veritable mine of wealth to escape their notice. But, with the usual disdain of high-class Hindus, they scorned to soil their hands with commerce.

And now, because all Parsee enterprise, jute mills are arising all along the Hoogly bank. Already they have made such progress (chiefly because of the nearness of raw jute and coal) that a generation hence they will wrest from the Dundee its entire Asiatic trade in jute.

Mr. R. D. Mehta, the pioneer of the concern, became one of the most distinguished citizens of Calcutta, and ultimately its Sheriff. And perhaps, following his venture, some other millionaire Parsee will now cross over from the Bombay side and give a new impetus to the working of the coal mines of Bengal. Then others will take up the iron in the Central Provinces, and the copper in Behar.

FEW, BUT VIGOROUS.

Why not? The commercial success of the Parsees is but a manifestation of a subtle law of economics, which postulates that "in a conservative community minorities must rise to the surface." Driven from Persia thirteen centuries ago by a religious persecution, the Parsees found an asylum in India. But though kindly received by the Hindus—they were indeed of the same Aryan race as the Hindus—the rigorous caste laws of the latter barred the possibility of intermarriage between them. Thus the Parsees remained small in number, but ever active, ever vigilant, ever looking for an opportunity for material progress.

LEADING PARSI OF CALCUTTA: DEATH OF MR. R. D. MEHTA
The Times of India (1861-current); Oct 23, 1930;
ProQuest Historical Newspapers: The Times of India (1838-2002)
pg. 10

LEADING PARSI OF CALCUTTA.

DEATH OF MR. R. D. MEHTA

Calcutta has lost a personality by the death of Mr. R. D. Mehta, C.I.E., who at the age of 81 died on Friday at 9, Rainey Park, Ballygunge.

Mr. Mehta was born in Bombay in July 1849, belonging to the *Shenshiah*, or the Imperial class. He was first educated at Bombay, but in 1860 he came to Calcutta and joined the Bengal Academy upon leaving which he was apprenticed to the firm of Messrs. Apcar and Co., In 1870 Mr. Mehta went to Hong Kong to inaugurate a branch of his father's business, and seven years later he went to England to purchase the machinery with which he founded the Empress Cotton Mill in Calcutta.

From that time he became closely identified with many other commercial and public enterprises which benefitted a large contingent of the poorer classes of Bengal. He paid several visits to England and he was the only member of the Parsi community on the deputation that went to Simla to present to the Viceroy the Address from the Princes and People of Bengal to Her Majesty the Queen Empress on the occasion of her Diamond Jubilee.

Mr. Mehta was nominated Sheriff of Calcutta in 1893 and it was at about that time that various attempts were made to do away with the office, which is a link between the official and non-official communities. During his term of office, Mr. Mehta successfully resisted its abolition.

C. I. E. CONFERRED.

In various capacities Mr. Mehta continued to make his influence and philanthropy felt, and with his remarkable success in business and perfect urbanity of manners he combined qualities that placed him in the front rank of Bengal's public men of the day. It was fitting therefore that the popularity with which his appointment as Sheriff was acclaimed should have found further and wider expression when in 1897 the dignity of "Companion of the Indian Empire", was conferred upon him. Mr. Mehta was entertained at dinner by a company of Europeans, Hindus, Parsis, and Mahomedans, Mr. Pugh, then leader of the Bar, presiding. On that occasion a speaker, referring to the letters comprising Mr. Mehta's name; remarked "M. stands for modesty: E. for energy; H. for honesty; T. for truthfulness; and A. for affability. I challenge any one who has come in contact with our friend to deny that he possesses these qualities in a superlative degree."

The late Sir Surendra Nath Banerjea pointed out that Mr. Mehta was the first Parsi in the metropolis of India to be decorated.

Even a brief list of Mr. Mehta's activities is sufficient to demonstrate the usefulness of his many-sided activities, and only one of his unbounded energy could in the midst of such a notable career have found time to add further to his reputation by establishing himself as a man of letters. He was the author of several books.

Mr. Mehta was a Life Member of the Asiatic Society of Bengal, a member of the Society of Arts, Governor of the Mayo Hospital; Vice-President of the British Indian Association, an Honorary Magistrate and Justice of the Peace, Chairman of Alipore Local Board since its formation in 1886 until 1918 and Chairman of the Manicktolla Municipality from 1900 until 1907.

THE VICE-CONSULAR CASE: THE ACCUSED CONVICTED THE ARTICLE AND THE CI
The Times of India (1861-current); Mar 8, 1901;
ProQuest Historical Newspapers: The Times of India (1838-2002)
pg. 3

THE VICE-CONSULAR CASE.

THE ACCUSED CONVICTED.

At the Esplanade Police Court, yesterday afternoon, Mr. J. Saunders Slater, Chief Presidency Magistrate, delivered his decision in the defamation case in which Mr. Cowasjee D. Rustomjee, late Vice-Consul for Persia in Bombay, charged Jalaludin Hooseini, a Moghul, with publishing certain allegations in his weekly Persian paper printed at Calcutta, and called the *Hablul Matin*.

Mr. Smetham, solicitor, appeared for the complainant. Mr. W. R. Hamilton, barrister-at-law, instructed by Mr. Mirza Hoosen Khan, solicitor, defended the accused.

THE ARTICLE AND THE CHARGES.

The Magistrate said that the article complained of appeared in the *Hablul Matin*, dated 29th January, 1900. It imputed, generally, shameful deeds and behaviour and criminal actions to the complainant Mr. Cowasjee, and was written avowedly for the purpose of procuring his dismissal from the Vice-Consulship. The accused had adopted the defence of justification, and in his defence had specified various charges against the complainant, namely:—(1) At Calcutta, he attempted to obtain a bribe from Mr. R. D. Mehta, C.I.E., to enlist his influence in obtaining the Persian Consular appointment at Calcutta; (2) he had begged for a sum of money from the Tagore family at Calcutta; (3) he had been guilty of breach of trust at Calcutta in respect of certain coins entrusted to him; (4) he had misappropriated a carpet at Bombay; (5) he had stolen or misappropriated a picture, the property of the Persian Consulate at Bombay; and (6) he had been masquerading in public at Bombay and elsewhere as a member of the Persian Order of the Sun and Lion not having been duly nominated a member to that order. The acqused having made those assertions, the burden of proving them fell upon him.

THE EVIDENCE AND THE CONCLUSIONS.

As to the first charge, the only evidence in support of it was that of Mr. R. D. Mehta. He said that the complainant had offered to him the Persian Consulship at Calcutta on condition that he was to bring forward Rs. 5,000 or Rs. 6,000 to be paid to and distributed by the complainant in any way the latter liked. Mr. Cowasjee denied the statements made by Mr. Mehta. He stated that it was Mr. Mehta who was anxious to oust his (the complainant's) cousin, Mr. Hirjibhoy, from the Consulship at Calcutta. He asked complainant's assistance in the matter, which he refused, and consequently incurred his animosity. But the fact remained that Mr. Mehta did obtain the Consulship, and he had said that he did not pay anything at all to obtain the post. A very significant fact was that Mr. Mehta admitted having paid before his appointment, and within a very few days of his first introduction to the Consul-a very few days of his first introduction to the Consul-General, for a victoria-phaeton, which the Consul-General had selected at Stewart and Co's place at Calcutta. No reason was advanced by Mr. Mehta for so handsome a gift, though he said that he gave it at complainant's suggestion. This was entirely inconsistent with Mr. Mehta's re-iterated statement that he had refused to incur any pecuniary obligation in connection with the Consulship. Mr. Mehta had, moreover, stated that he was not on favourabl[illegible] at the time the matter w[illegible]deration, the Court [illegible] charge, and acc[illegible] true. It followed [illegible] out this charge a[illegible] failed to make out the charges in relation to the begging for money from the Raja Surendronath Tagore, the alleged embezzlement of coins at Calcutta, and the misappropriation of the carpet. With regard to the alleged stealing of the Consulate picture, the Court held that it was the property of the late Consul-General, who gave it to the complainant

THE ORDER OF THE SUN AND LION.

The Court believed the complainant's statement that he had received the *firman* appointing him a member to the Order of the Sun and Lion by his Imperial Majesty the Shah of Persia, from the Consul-General of Persia, and that it was a genuine *firman*. As regarded the Star, it seemed improbable that the Vice-Consul should take into his confidence, for the purchase of such a conspicuous article as the Star of a Persian Order, one of the Consul-General's domestic servant receiving ten rupees a month. But further than that, it seemed absolutely beyond the bounds of possibility that the Vice-Consul would venture to appear at a public function, at which the Consul-General for Persia and a large number of gentlemen well acquainted with Persian affairs were present, wearing on his breast a Star resembling a Star of the Order of the Sun and Lion he was not entitled to wear, and that no notice should have been taken by anyone of such contempt of an Imperial Order. Whether the Star belonged to the Military or the Civil Division was of no importance in this case, supposing that it was duly granted to the complainant. But if it was not the particular design which, as a Civil member, the complainant was entitled to wear, it would attract additional notice, and the complainant would render himself the more likely to be called upon to explain its possession. No such explanation was called for. The Court held that at the time of the illuminations made in honour of the Shah, the complainant was a member of the Order; the Star he wore on the occasion was duly conferred upon him; and the charges made against him in this respect were unfounded.

THE CONVICTION AND THE SENTENCE.

The defence had not shown that either before publication of the article or since the institution of the proceedings, the accused had taken the least care or trouble to ascertain whether his statements regarding the complainant were true or untrue. The accused himself had not, nor had his counsel for him, suggested that he had made any enquiry whatever as to the truth of anyone of those six allegations.

THE DECISION.

The charge framed by the Court against the accused was proved. The article itself showed the animosity which the accused had displayed towards the complainant. He had mentioned five methods by which he attempted to bring discredit upon the complainant and his dismissal. The failure of each of those five attempts should have caused him to hesitate before he renewed his attempts in his newspaper. But he not only published his article, but for more than twelve months after that he continued and intensified his libel, and the last effort of his counsel in the hearing of the case was an emphatic reiteration of those charges. The complainant had to meet those charges and to refute them. He had done so, and had, in the opinion of the Court, come through this protracted and malicious litigation with the greatest credit. But it was necessary to deter proprietors of newspapers from inflicting such grievous hardships upon unoffending persons. The accused was, therefore, sentenced to three months' simple imprisonment in the Common Prison, and to pay a fine of Rs. 1,000. In default of payment of the fine, he should undergo further simple imprisonment for six months. Out of the fine, if paid, Rs. 750 was ordered to be paid to the complainant.

SOME FRIENDLY MOGHULS.

Some Bombay Moghuls, who were Persian subjects, were present in Court to learn the result of the case. When the decision was made known to them, they warmly congratulated Mr. Cowasjee, and his solicitor, Mr. Smetham, as they both walked into the corridor. They also wanted to present garlands and bouquots. Both the gentlemen, however, declined to be party to such a demonstration, and they succeeded, after some persuasion, in inducing their over-zealous friends to walk out of the Court premises quietly.

BOMBAY POLICE COURTS.

THE VICE-CONSULAR CASE.

At the Esplanade Police Court, Bombay, before Mr. J. Sanders Slater, Chief Presidency Magistrate, yesterday afternoon, the charge of defamation made by Mr. Cowasjee D. Rustomjee, lately Vice-Consul for Persia in Bombay, against Jalaludin Husein, the editor of a Calcutta Persian weekly, called the *Habl-ul Matin*, was called on for further inquiry.

Mr F. Soratjee Taleyarkhan, instructed by Mr. Smetham, appeared for the complainant, and Mr. W. R. Hamilton, instructed by Mr. Mirza Hoosein Khan, defended the accused.

AN OFFICIAL DOCUMENT.

Mr. Taleyarkhan said that the complainant's solicitors, Messrs. Smetham, Bland, and Noble, had received a letter from Mr. W. T. Morison, Secretary to the Bombay Government, Political Department. It stated that in continuation of the letter of the 24th December, 1900, he had to say that the British Legation at Teheran had intimated to the Government of India, on the 2nd January, 1901, at the request of the Persian Government, that a Persian firman and decoration of the Sun and the Lion had been officially conferred on Mr. Cowasjee D. Rustomjee. Mr. Taleyarkhan inquired of the Magistrate whether the Court had received a reply to the communication it had been kind enough to make to the Government direct.

The Magistrate said that he had received a copy from the Government of the letter addressed to the solicitors.

Mr. Taleyarkhan applied that the document being an official record might form part of the proceedings.

Mr. Hamilton objected to its going in as evidence. The particular section in the Evidence Act treating of the admissibility of "foreign records" was Section 75, the provisions of which were not complied with in the present instance. It was not an act of the executive published in the Court Journal or Gazette of Persia by authority, nor was it a copy certified under the seal of Persia or of its sovereign, nor was it a recognition thereof in some public act of the Governor-General of India in Council. In fact, it was only a letter from the Local Government.

Mr. Taleyarkhan contended that the document came under Section 35 of the Act, it being an entry in a public or official book, register, or record.

Mr Hamilton said that the section cited by his learned friend applied only to British records and not to foreign records.

After considerable discussion, the Magistrate ruled that had he received the letter from the Government of India it would have been admissible under Section 78.

Mr. Taleyarkhan applied for time to enable the prosecution to reach the Government of India, and obtain an authoritative certified statement from their register finally on the point. If the Court considered it necessary he would even go to the length of asking for the issue of a commission to Teheran; but, of course, that would mean a delay of about a couple of months.

The Magistrate said that it was not a matter in which such a long postponement at the closing of a case was desirable.

Mr. Taleyarkhan made another application. He said he wanted to adduce, with the Court's permission, further evidence to show that the decoration of the order, in which the Lion was standing, was not necessarily a military order. There were several recipients of it who were not military, but were civil officials, notable among whom was the present Consul-General for Persia in India.

Mr. Hamilton said that the Consul-General had admitted to him personally that he was a General in the Persian Army. In that event, his decoration must have been essentially of a military character, with a standing lion and not a sitting lion.

The Magistrate did not think it desirable to extend the inquiry on that point further at such a late stage.

ADDRESS FOR THE DEFENCE.

Mr. Hamilton then summed up the case for the defence. He regretted that the case had taken such a long time to come. But he said that much of the delay could be laid at the door of the prosecution, who, when his Worship went to Europe on leave lengthened out the proceedings in some way or the other. They even went to the length of consulting the Advocate-General, who, however, gave them very good advice. That officer informed them that, although it was very desirable to have a case decided by the Magistrate who had heard the most of the evidence, there was nothing to present the decision of the case being given by another Magistrate, who happened to be acting in the post of the Magistrate who had heard the evidence, during the latter's absence. It would, therefore, appear that for the prolongation of the proceedings the defence were in no way to be blamed. As regarded the accused, he did not know the complainant Mr. Cowasjee except by sight. He knew that Mr. Cowasjee was Vice-Consul, and besides meeting him and salaaming him on one or two occasions, he hardly knew anything more of that gentleman. Such a man could never be said to have been actuated by motives of animosity against the party to whom he had no cause to offer any enmity. The accused was editor of a paper. He edited it so well and wrote it in such classical and pure Persian that his own Government had bestowed on him the designation of the "Truthful," besides conferring on him a distinction in recognition of his literary labours. On the other hand, what was the complainant's position? He called himself a commission agent, dealing in diamonds and precious stones. The "commission agent," was, in counsel's opinion, nothing more or less than a broker. If this was the complainant's regular business, by which he earned five or six thousand rupees a year, where were the books of accounts which contained his transactions? Where were the receipts of the income-tax he had paid? He was not a rich man. According to the evidence he had applied to the Persian Government for payment of salary for the post of Vice-Consul, which had been held to be a place of honour, and not one carrying with it remuneration. In reply, he got in lieu of about his ten years' service only Rs. 700, which came to a very small amount per month. It was in evidence that he had been dismissed from his post: he had not resigned it. The fact of his dismissal still stood unaltered and uncancelled. Mr. Mehta's evidence was clear about him. But then he had said that Mr. Mehta was bitterly hostile to him. It was alleged that because of those inimical feelings the attack was published in the articles complained of. First of all, counsel contended there was no attack at all. Whatever action was taken by the accused was taken by him openly and regularly. It was proved that the accused was in possession of some letters, which he forwarded to the Consul-General.

He believed that somehow or other Mr. Cowasjee was not a proper person for the Vice-Consulship. On this honest belief he acted. Finding that the Consul-General, who was Mr. Cowasjee's superior officer, did not deal with the matter, he assumed his functions of a responsible editor, and began informing the public. In that he had discharged his duty to his king and country. He narrated in his columns what steps he had taken to bring the facts he was in possession of to the notice of the Consul-General, who had lawful authority over Mr Cowasjee. He said that Mr. Cowasjee did not preserve the honour and dignity of his post. By no sort of travesty could such open conduct on the part of the accused be construed into making malicious accusations. He made the statement for the public good, and followed it up in Court by producing evidence in support of what he had said. In the case for the defence, there were three points in which evidence had been called regarding transactions in Bombay. Two more points related to affairs in Calcutta. Among the Bombay points was the incident of the Persian carpet, the value of which, sixty rupees, Mr. Cowasjee had used for himself. The second point pertained to the picture. There was a specific writing on the picture that it was an official article, specially intended for the Consulate at Bombay. Mr. Cowasjee took it for his own use. Mr. Cowasjee's explanation about it was that the Consul-General had presented it to him. The third point was the star of the decoration. Great suspicion attached to the decoration. No public meeting was convened to confer it; no newspaper accounts were published; nor were congratulations showered. If at all it was given to him, it was a sorry affair, a hole-and-corner affair. The man who had a decoration like that would have been as proud as a peacock. But the defence had contended all along, and it said still, that there was nothing to shew that the order had been conferred on Mr. Cowasjee. No account of its conference appeared in the *Iran*, the Court paper of Persia. No certified entry was forthcoming from the register of the Persian Foreign Office or from the records of the Persian Consulate in India testifying to its conference. The firman was not a properly drawn up, illuminated, attested, and sealed document. Coming to the points of the transactions transpiring in Calcutta, counsel said that the first was disclosed in Mr Mehta's evidence. Mr. Mehta was one of the most leading men in Calcutta. He had said that when Mr Cowasjee offered him the appointment of Vice-Consulship, Mr. Cowasjee asked of him five or six thousand rupees. Twice did he reject the offer on such terms. Eventually the Consul-General himself came to him with it, and he gave it to him without asking for any money. It was impossible that a man of Mr Mehta's standing could tell an untruth in that. But Mr. Cowasjee had alleged against him enmity—bitter enmity. It was certainly Mr. Mehta's misfortune to know Mr. Cowasjee from a boy, but as to his bearing any ill-will or animosity against Mr. Cowasjee there was no cause. The other point that bore against Mr. Cowasjee in the Calcutta business was the money transaction with the Tagores, in respect of the Vice-Consulship there. Against the express evidence tendered by the defence in support of that fact there was the barest denial on paper by the Tagore solicitors. That paper, however, was not much in value as evidence. No denial was made on oath; there was no cross-examination of the witness making that denial in Court. Such evidence was not worth any consideration. In conclusion, counsel said that the defence had proved by means of good and reliable evidence, that the accused was justified in making the statements he had published in his newspaper. This he had done in his *rôle* of a respectable journalist, and for the benefit of the Persian Government.

The hearing was adjourned for Mr. Taleyarkhan's address.

ADULTERATED GHEE.—At the Mazagon Police Court, before Mr. W. Webb, Velji Nanji, Jethabai, his wife, and Dharamsi Ratansi, his servant, were charged, at the instance of Dr. Sorabjee Cowasjee Divisional Health Officer, with selling an article as ghee, which, on analysis, was found not to contain substances exclusively derived from milk.—Mr. Leslie Crawford, Solicitor to the Bombay Municipality, appeared for the prosecution. Mr. Oliveira, pleader, defended the accused.—For the first accused it was contended that he was not at the shop when the ghee was sold. He was discharged.—The Magistrate remarked that as the two remaining accused appeared to have been ignorant of the regulations regarding ghee, and had sold the ghee as they had purchased it from a vendor, they were sentenced to pay a nominal penalty of five rupees each.

ROBBING AN EMPLOYER.—At the Mazagon Police Court, yesterday, before Mr. W. Webb, Presidency Magistrate, Wazirulla Hasan, servant to Shewshunkerlal, was charged with committing criminal breach of trust in respect of Rs. 101, belonging to his employer.—The evidence showed that the complainant, who has his shop in Bhendy Bazaar, entrusted the money to the accused for the purpose of sending a remittance to Cawnpore but the accused misappropriated the money and decamped to Cawnpore, which is his native place. On a report being made to the Bombay police, measures were adopted for the accused's arrest at Cawnpore on arrival. It seemed, however, that the accused returned to Bombay by the return train, presumably on his having learnt of the instructions wired for his apprehension, and surrendered himself to his master, who handed him over to Inspector Barker.—He was sentenced to three months' rigorous imprisonment.

CONTRARY TO REGULATIONS.—At the Esplanade Police Court, yesterday, before Mr. P. H. Dastur, Balia, Kamalia and Zilloo tindals, were charged with contravening the plague rules.—Mr. Nicholson, Public Prosecutor, prosecuted.—The accused were alleged to have taken passengers to Karanja without having them medically examined under the rules, or without submitting the crew of their boats to a similar inspection.—The case against the first accused was adjourned for the purpose of finding out the real tindal of the boat.—The second accused was fined one rupee for each passenger carried in his boat, in all Rs. 21.—The third accused's defence was that while he was away from the boat to obtain the doctor's certificate his crew sailed with the boat. He called one of his crew as a witness in substantiation of the statement.—The Magistrate gave him the benefit of the doubt, and discharged him.

APPENDIX II

Tawarikhe-Dastoor Jamasp Ashana
(History of the Jamasp Ashana Family)
Translation from Gujarati by Homi D Patel

Sardar Dastur Kaikobad Aaderbad

With the end of the history of this Dasturji, the history of the descendants of the Late Dastur Behmanji Jamshedji ends here. He was the youngest son of Dastur Behramji – the fourth son of the first Head Dastur of the Deccan – Dastur Jamaspji Edulji, but since his paternal cousin the Late Ervad Aderbad was adopted by Dastoor Nosherwan, he is associated with his name. He was born at the Dastur hall at Poona on Roj 11th Mah 2nd 1231 Yezdezardi dated 3rd November 1861, Samvat 1918's Kartik Sud 1 (date according to Hindu calendar), it was a Sunday. He acquired the training of "Naaver Martaab" (i.e. training to be initiated into priesthood) under the able guidance of his maternal uncle and then on Roj 22nd Mah 7th Yezdezardi 1243 dated 10th April 1874, Samvat 1930 acquired the advance training of Ervad at the main Dehermeher of Navsari. Under the guidance of the same teacher, he studied further and did the advance study of "Paav Mahal" and "Barashnum". He followed the profession of "Yozdathragiri" for quite a long time. He was trained in Marathi, Farsi and English languages at Poona's Government High School, and studied Sanskrit under one Pandit. He achieved excellence in the languages of "Zend" and "Pehelvi" by taking up its advance studies under the guidance of his able paternal uncle Late Sardar Dastur Hoshang Jamasp.

Right from his childhood, he had inculcated hobby of drawing portraits, and he gradually developed that ability in him. Many a portrait, drawn by him still adorn his present day residence, giving the idea of his artistic brush.

After his appointment as the Head Dastur of the Deccan, the prominent ceremonies performed by him included the laying of the foundation and bringing into the service – the "Dokhma" at Igatpuri. The foundation laying of the aforesaid "Dokhma" was performed with the help of his maternal uncle, Dastur Khurshedji Jamshedji of Mhow under the supervision of his elder paternal uncle – Late Sardar Dastur Nosherwanji Jamespji – on Roj 19th Maha 8th in the year 1253 Yezdezardi dated 4th May 1884. Thereafter, the ceremony of "Parthavani" – i.e. consecration – was performed under the supervision of his second (the Gujarati word used here could also mean "Other") paternal uncle, Sardar Dastur Hoshang Jamasp on Roj 16th Mah 9th in the year 1254 Yezdezardi dated 31st May 1885. The Anjuman of Igatpuri felicitated him with a Shawl, on his accomplishment.

He was appointed the Head Dasturji, on the day of the "Uthamna ceremony" (the third day's ritual since the demise of a Parsi Zoroastrian) of his eldest Paternal uncle, the Late Sardar Dastur Nosherwanji Jamaspji – which was on Roj 12th Mah 2nd in the year 1254 Yezdezardi, dated 29th October 1884. Five shawls from the following greeted his appointment:

1. From the Trustees of the Late Sheth Sohrabji Rattanji Patel's Charitable Trust.
2. From the Anjuman of Poona.
3. From Dastur Jamshedji Rustomji Jamasp Aasha.
4. From Sheth Hormusji Sohrabji Todiwalla.
5. From Sheth Dhunjishaw Jamshedji Ankleshsaria.

During March 1895, he was appointed as a Government nominated member at the Municipal Corporation of Poona and presently he adorns the post of its vice chairman.

Before being appointed as the Head Priest, he published many books. In June 1896, he translated "Karname Ardeshir Babegan" from Pehlvi to English and Gujarati and published it along with the original narration of "The Shahanama". Thereafter in December 1899, he published "Jande Behmanyesht" with its Pehlvi text and Gujarati translation and the translation of "Mino Khered" from Paazend to Gujarati. The Pehlvi text of "Behman Yasht" was printed by the "Photozinco Process". All the above three books received critical appreciation from English and Gujarati newspapers.

"Mr. Cama Memorial Volume" which was edited by Shamshul Olma Ervad Jivanji Jamshedji Modi in the year 1901, as a token of remembrance on the seventy-first birthday of the late scholar Sheth Khurshedji Rustomji Cama – included "Avesta Shabde No Mool" (The origin of the word Avesta) a write up by him. The famous scholar of the Pehelvi Language – Doctor West – termed that write up as "--- of requiring extreme attention". The issue of the magazine "Raast Goftar" dated 8th September 1901, carried the following citation:-

"Dastur Kaikobad Noshirwan Jamasp Aashana, has undertaken a very informative topic of exploring the root of Avasta and we are of the opinion that he has more or less reached the point of success; so also will be acknowledged by our Parsi as well European Scholars."

During July 1903, the Honourable Government granted him the respect of appointing him the Honorary Magistrate of Poona.

The "Parthavani ceremony" of the Dokhmas at Devlali was accomplished solely by himself on Roj 19th Maha 3rd in the year 1277 Yezdezardi on date 1st December 1907, on that day he was honoured by the Anjuman of that place, by bestowing a shawl. Thereafter he set out to inspect the : Panthaks (undertaking of offering religious services by junior mobeds) under him and had to visit Bhusaval, Akola, Badnera, Nagpur, Kamli and Igatpuri. At all those places, he received pomp welcome along with scrolls of honour and shawls. Some gents also arranged for a function of tea party.

He ascended the throne of High Priest of Deccan of Roj 15th and Maha 8th in the year 1277 Yezdezardi dated 25th April 1908, after the demise of Sardar Dastur Hoshang Jamasp. A resolution supporting his appointment, made on behalf of the Trustees of the Late Sheth Sohorabji Rattanji Patel's Charitable Trust was read out before the Anjuman – which was as follows:-

"Gentlemen of the Anjuman, The Trustees of the Late Sheth Sohorabji Rattanji Patel's Dehermeher and Charitable Trust, note with utter grief the sad demise of one of our Co-trustee and the Head Priest of this Dehermeher – Dastur Hoshangji, who during the course of his life had brought about a progress in facilities at this Dehermeher and all the charitable trusts by his tireless efforts and that is how they have been able to reach the present state of excellence. Now, in accordance of the authority vested in us – the existing trustees – by the Trust deed and by consensus, nominate our present assistant Dastur Kaikobad Saheb Aaderbad Dastur Nosherwan in place of the Late Dasturji Saheb Hosangji for the management of the Dehermeher and keeping updated all the arrangements. We sincerely hope that our Anjuman will also like this appointment. The Late Dasturji Hoshangji's dedication of his entire long life to his pious post and by the ardent services offered had won over the hearts of all; Dastur Kaikobad will also follow in his auspicious steps and will give sufficient satisfaction to the Trustees as well as the Anjuman, of that we are very much sure.

We are very much sure that the way in which the administration of this Dasturi throne was taken care of during the time of the Late Dasturji, Dasturji Kaikobad will also have the same style of functioning and the affection of the Anjuman will keep on increasing his happiness. We the present Trustees – with some anticipation and assurance – feel the previously mentioned appointment to be fit.

Dastur Kaikobad had acquired quite an art and gained a vast experience having functioned as an assistant to the Late Dastur Saheb Hoshangji. In the similar manner, with a view to keep up the tradition of this Dasturi throne, we trustees have arranged for the son of Dastur Kaikobad, Bhai Nosherwan – who is presently under extensive training – that after he completes his training he will be appointed as the assistant Dastur. We believe this arrangement will also meet the approval of our Anjuman.

After the reading of the above resolution, and after the conclusion of "the Uthamna Ceremony" of Dastur Hoshangji – he started being greeted upon his being appointed the Head Priest – during the course of the greetings the following seventy five honoured him with a shawl.

(List of seventy-five that was to be avoided)

Within only three months after ascending the throne – that is during July 1908 the Honourable Government bestowed upon him the title of the First Grade Sardar of the Deccan and by virtue of that, his inclusion was made in the Levy that is held in the Government Palaces. The excellent quality of Dasturi and his nobleness was highly appreciated in the Government circles and he was conferred the title of "Private Honorary". The manner in which this honour was carried in the English as well as Gujarati newspapers – will be appropriate – if mentioned here: -

"The Head Priest of Deccan Dastur Kaikobad Aaderbad Dastur Nosherwanji has been appointed as the Sardar of the 1st grade by the Honourable Government. The rank of a Head Priest should be considered more then any other Governmental honours despite this fact the Parsis of Poona and Deccan will not be able to conceal their joy upon the achievements of their Head Priest. Dastur Kaikobad is truly worthy of this honour.

*** He has given substantive services in the legislative assembly also. ***

"We convey our heartiest greetings to Dasturji Saheb Kaikobad for such a magnificent achievement and wish that he keeps on getting more and more such adornments"

(Jam-e Jamshed: 21st July 1908)

In the Parsi community presently there are three Baronets, two Knights and a Sardar and to that there is the addition of one more Sardar. The Honourable position of the Head Priest of the Parsis of Deccan and Malwa has been graced since many years by the descendents of Dastur Jamesp Aashana. Two Dastur Sahebs – the last of this clan – Dastur Nosherwanji Jamaspji and his brother Dastur Hoshangji held the position of the first grade of the Dasturs. Presently their successor, the new Dastur Kaikobad Aaderbad has also been conferred with the honour of being decorated as the Sardar of the first grade by the Honourable Government and has spread joy and cheers in the community. We have been observing that this Dasturi family of Poona has won the laurels and honours because of their wisdom, ability and determination. The native place of that family is Navsari and as a rule, the Athornan tribe of Navsari has been a success wherever they have been because of the wisdom of their heart. However, the Jamesp Aasha family of Poona have gained their fame due to their knowledge of the religion, their progressive habits in keeping with the current trends, and considering it as their ardent duty to make their fellow tribesmen achieve progress. Dasturs could be found in plenty today, but those that guide their tribe in accordance of the advanced knowledge of their religion to stride on the true path, are not known to us to be found except – those daring Dasturs from Poona.

* * * Dasturs should of course be of clean conscience and of advanced knowledge * * *

Dastur Kaikobad had a pragmatic mentality; he was an archenemy of superstition, fanatics and obstinacy and believes in keeping up the pace of progress along with the world. We heartily congratulate such a religious scholar for having achieved the rank of a Sardar from the Government. [italics mine]
(Raast Goftar – 26th July 1908).

The presentation ceremony of the scroll was presided over by the Agent of the Sardars – Mr. Ropar on 22nd July 1910, the day that was also celebrated as the birthday of His Highness the King, at a pompous gathering at a Darbar at Poona.

He was appointed to preside over a Zarthoshty conference called by some prominent Zoroastrians in Bombay, on 16th April 1910. An agitation arose amongst the Parsis, as a couple of Bombay based Parsi newspapers tried to create a hindrance to holding such a meeting and quite an effort had been made by them for creating an obstacle. However, due to the perseverance, patience, tact and far-sightedness of the organisers they overcame this hindrance and the conference was successfully held. Whilst delivering the Presidential address, the Dasturji impressed the crowd so much by use of his rational and mature words, that they created a miraculous effect on the audience. After hearing the lecture, an arch opponent who was against this conference right from the beginning – an eminent Sheth of Bombay – Sheth Shapurji Behramji Katrak, even dared to withdraw his earlier hostility. Not only that, but in order to laud that conference, a dinner was arranged on the night of 30th April at the Grant Road bungalow of Sheth Nusserwanji Maneckji Petit which was presided over by Sir Dinshaw Maneckji Petit Baronet.

The performance of the consecration ceremony of the Adarian at the Madras Dehermeher on Roj 29th Maha 11 1279 Yezdezerdi on 7th August 1910 under his leadership. On that occasion, the Anjuman of that place – with a scroll of honour and a shawl, graced him. During that occasion, he took a chance to call upon the Government of Madras Sir Arthur Lolly at the Government Palace resort in Oatacommud.

On 17th November 1910 the Honourable Government appointed him as a delegate of "Parsi District Matrimonial Court".

[*Tawarikhe-Dastoor Jamasp Ashana* (Bombay: Mumbai Vartaman Press, 1912), 146-53.]

Translation from Gujarati by Homi D Patel

REFERENCES

'A Conference of Living Religions London.' 1924. Report by Thomas Albert Howard.

'Trust Deed - Late D B Mehta Zoroastrian Anjuman Atash Adaran'.

1912. *Tawarikhe-Dastoor Jamasp Ashana* [History of the Jamasp Ashana family]. Bombay: Mumbai Vartaman Press.

2005. *Judgments: Petit vs Jeejeebhoy 1908 and Saklat vs Bella 1925*. Bombay: Parsiana Publications.

2011. *75 Years of Service: Calcutta Zoroastrian Stree Mandal.*

A Century in Time: Celebrating the Centenary [1912-2012] of the Late Ervad Dhunjeebhoy Byramjee Mehta's Zoroastrian Anjuman Atash Adaran, Kolkata.

Banaji, Khoshru Navroji. 1892. *Memoirs of the late Framji Cawasji Banaji.*

Bhave, SR. 1970. *Saga of Security: Story of Indian Life Insurance.* Life Insurance Corporation of India.

Darukhanawala, HD. 1939. *Parsi Lustre on Indian Soil.*

Dastur Sheriarji Dadabhai Bharucha. Dastur Hoshang Memorial volume. 'Is Zoroastrianism Preached to all Mankind or to one Particular Race.'

Desai, SM. *Mehta Vansavali.*

Desai, Sohrabji Mancherji. *Twarikhe Navsari* [History of Parsis of Navsari].

Famous Parsis: Biographical and Critical Sketches. Madras: Natesan & Co.

Haug, Martin. 1907. *Essays on the Sacred Language, Writings, and Religion of the Parsis*. London: Kegan Paul, Trench, Trubner & Co Ltd.

Kotwal, Firoze M. 2017. Vol. 1, No. 3 – 'An Overview of the History and Development of the Parsi Priesthood in India upto the 19th century'. Samuel Jordan Center for Persian Studies and Culture, University of California, Irvine.

Kulke, Eckhard. 1974. *The Parsees in India. A Minority as Agent of Social Change.* Munchen: Weltforum Verlag.

Lala, RM. 2017. *Beyond the Last Blue Mountain – A Life of JRD Tata.* Penguin Random House India.

Mills, Lawrence. *Our Own Religion in Ancient Persia.*

Nanavutty, Piloo. 1977. *The Parsis.*

Navroji, Dadabhoy. 1861. *The Parsee Religion*. University of London.

Our Own Little Piece of Earth: Calcutta Parsee Club 1908 - 2008

Patel, Dinyar. 2012. 'RD Mehta (1849 -1930): A Leading Calcutta Parsi'. https://dinyarpatel.com/2012/09/24/r-d-mehta-1849-1930-a-leading-calcutta-parsi/

———. 2016. 'The Banaji and Mehta Families: Forging the Parsi Community in Calcutta.' In *Holy Wealth: Accounting for this World and the Next in Religious Belief and Practice (Festschrift for John R. Hinnells),* ed. Almut Hintze and Alan Williams, pp. 211-30. Wiesbaden: Harrassowitz Verlag.

Petit Vs Jeejeebhoy in the High Court of Juridicture at Bombay. Suit No. 689 of 1906, 27 November 1908.

Rodrigues, Louiza. 2014. *The Genealogy of the Sett and Sethna Families.* Mumbai. K R Cama Oriental Institute.

Saklat vs Bella Privy Council Records 1925, No 88: volume 24 [JCPC Suit No 57 of 1924].

Saklat vs Bella. Suit No 91 of 1915 of the Chief Court of Lower Burma.

Sharafi, Mitra. 2010. *Colonial Parsis and Law - A Cultural History - Government Research Fellowship Lectures 2009-2010.* Mumbai: K R Cama Oriental Institute.

———. *Bella's Case: Parsi Identity and Law in Colonial Rangoon, Bombay and London.*

———. *Law and Identity in Colonial South Asia: Parsi Legal Culture 1772-1947.*

Taraporewala, JS Erach. 1993. *The Gathas: The Divine Songs of Zarathushtra.* Bombay: Hukhta Foundation.

Tata Central Archives

The Iran League Quarterly. Official Organ of the Iran League, Bombay.

ACKNOWLEDGEMENTS

First and foremost I am grateful to Mr Noshir Tankariwala who advised me, 'this book is an absolute must, to be published, not only for the present generation's enlightenment and knowledge but for posterity.' I am thankful to him for reading my first manuscript in minute detail and giving me the confidence to complete the book.

The panthak of the Late Ervad D.B. Mehta's Zoroastrian Anjuman Atash Adaran, Ervad Jimmy Taraporewala, gave me the idea to write a book on all the research I had done. He wanted some books on the Parsis of Calcutta to show to the groups of people who came to the Agiari in the morning on The Heritage Walks.

In these two years of looking back into history I have to thank historian Mitra Sharafi of the University of Wisconsin Law School for sharing the entire case file of Saklat Vs Bella, which she had obtained from the Privy Council Archives.

Dinyar Patel, the research scholar, shared Dadabhai Naoroji's letters and the old press cuttings and guided me in my research.

I must acknowledge the assistance from Ratan Tata in having the 'Sooni (Susaune Briere) Tata letters to her mother' authenticated by the Tata Central Archives.

My sister-in-law Shirin Mehta edited my original book, made many changes and gave me this final product. She converted a document of facts into a story. Thanks, Shirin, for all the time you spared and the effort you took for me.

A special thanks to June Jacobs who typed and retyped and corrected and re-corrected the manuscript.

Thank you to Jehangir Patel and Farrokh Jijina of Parsiana Publications who never tired of answering all my questions and to Mr Bikash De Niyogi who gave me the confidence to publish the book. When I was wondering how, why and what would go into publishing this book, his reply was – 'Just give me your manuscript'.

Mr Swaroop Mukerji, my friend, who always steps in to help when I need his artistic talent. He designed the beautiful cover of the Parsi priests crossing the old Howrah Bridge, carrying the holy 'alaat'.

Last but not the least Ms Sucharita Ghosh who edited my book.